1

all
tall
stall
install
installment

Sequential Spelling

Student Workbook

ISBN: 9781935943075

Day 1

Spelling Lesson:

As you hear them, write the spelling words for the day in the space provided. Be sure that you correct any words you have spelled incorrectly.

1. _____

2. _____

3. _____

4. _____

Using Your Words:

Sound-alike words

in\inn

Use a dictionary to find the meanings of these two words. Write one sentence using both words.

1._____

_____

2._____

_____

Day 2

Spelling Lesson:

As you hear them, write the spelling words for the day in the space provided. Be sure that you correct any words you have spelled incorrectly.

1. _____

2. _____

3. _____

4. _____

5. _____

6. _____

7. _____

8. _____

Using Your Words:

Sound-alike words

I\eye\aye

Use a dictionary to find the meanings of these words. Use them in a sentence with other words on your spelling list.

1._____

_____

2._____

_____

3._____

_____

Spelling Lesson:

As you hear them, write the spelling words for the day in the space provided. Be sure that you correct any words you have spelled incorrectly.

1._____

2._____

3._____

4._____

5._____

6._____

7._____

8._____

9._____

10. _____

11. _____

12. _____

Using Your Words:

Fill in the blanks with words from today's spelling list.

1. _____ hurt my sh _____!

2. She _____ the picture on the bulletin board.

3. Do you want to _____my friend?

4. First one to cross home plate _____ the game!

Spelling Lesson:

As you hear them, write the spelling words for the day in the space provided. Be sure that you correct any words you have spelled incorrectly.

1._____

2._____

3._____

4._____

5._____

6._____

7._____

8._____

9._____

10. _____

11. _____

12. _____

13. _____

14. _____

15. _____

16. _____

Using Your Words:

Sound-alike words:

we\wee
see\sea

Use a dictionary to find the meanings of these words. Use them in a sentence with other words on your spelling list.

1._____

_____

2._____

_____

3._____

_____

4._____

_____

Day 5

As you hear them, write the spelling words for the day in the space provided. Be sure that you correct any words you have spelled incorrectly.

1. _____

2. _____

3. _____

4. _____

5. _____

6. _____

7. _____

8. _____

9. _____

10. _____

11. _____

12. _____

13. _____

14. _____

15. _____

16. _____

17. _____

18. _____

19. _____

20. _____

Using Your Words:

Fill in the blanks with words from today's spelling list.

1. The be _____ of the game is the first _____.

2. She is th _____ than Susan.

3. He ch _____ himself ten times.

4. Subway rides are _____ after six p.m.

5. You are the w _____!

Day 6

Spelling Lesson:

As you hear them, write the spelling words for the day in the space provided. Be sure that you correct any words you have spelled incorrectly.

1. _____

2. _____

3. _____

4. _____

5. _____

6. _____

7. _____

8. _____

9. _____

10. _____

11. _____

12. _____

13. _____

14. _____

15. _____

16. _____

17. _____

18. _____

19. _____

20. _____

Using Your Words:

Fill in the blanks with words from today's spelling list.

1. We went to dinner at an _____.

2. My grandmother used to _____ a _____ keeper.

3. How many _____ are in a swarm?

4. Let's hope that driver _____ the turn!

5. Do you know anyone who had to _____ from injustice?

Day 7

Spelling Lesson:

As you hear them, write the spelling words for the day in the space provided. Be sure that you correct any words you have spelled incorrectly.

1. _____

2. _____

3. _____

4. _____

5. _____

6. _____

7. _____

8. _____

9. _____

10. _____

11. _____

12. _____

13. _____

14. _____

15. _____

16. _____

17. _____

18. _____

19. _____

20. _____

Using Your Words:

Fill in the blanks with words from today's spelling list.

1. A small child can be called a _____ babe.

2. Hello! Come _____, please and sit down.

3. Did that _____ sting hurt?

4. How did your sister like her stay at the _____?

5. I am a _____ at knitting.

6. _____ are winning the game.

Day 8

Spelling Lesson:

As you hear them, write the spelling words for the day in the space provided. Be sure that you correct any words you have spelled incorrectly.

1. _____

2. _____

3. _____

4. _____

5. _____

6. _____

7. _____

8. _____

9. _____

10. _____

11. _____

12. _____

13. _____

14. _____

15. _____

1.6. ._____

17. _____

18. _____

19. _____

20. _____

Using Your Words:

Sound-alike words

sees\seas
flees\fleas

Use a dictionary to find the meanings of these words. Use them in a sentence with other words on your spelling list.

1._____

_____

2._____

_____

3._____

_____

4._____

_____

Day 9

Spelling Lesson:

As you hear them, write the spelling words for the day in the space provided. Be sure that you correct any words you have spelled incorrectly.

1. _____

2. _____

3. _____

4. _____

5. _____

6. _____

7. _____

8. _____

9. _____

10. _____

11. _____

12. _____

13. _____

14. _____

15. _____

16. _____

17. _____

18. _____

19. _____

20. _____

21. _____

22. _____

23. _____

24. _____

25. _____

Using Your Words:

Fill in the blanks with words from today's spelling list.

1. Would you like a _____ of coffee?

2. It's hard to be in a good _____ early in the morning.

3. What's _____ with you?

4. The football game was a _____.

5. _____ 66 is a very famous road.

6. Please take _____ the trash. Thank you!

7. What is your favorite _____?

8. I have something in my _____.

9. Tim is just getting over a _____ of the flu.

10. Oak is a very hard _____.

Day 10

As you hear them, write the spelling words for the day in the space provided. Be sure that you correct any words you have spelled incorrectly.

1._____

2._____

3._____

4._____

5._____

6._____

7._____

8._____

9._____

10. _____

11. _____

12. _____

13. _____

14. _____

15. _____

16. _____

17. _____

18. _____

19._____

20. _____

21. _____

22. _____

23. _____

24. _____

25. _____

Using Your Words:

Unscramble these:

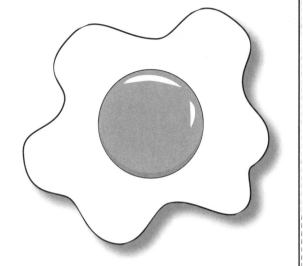

1. ulodw _____

2. oomd _____

3. oust _____

4. souert _____

5. doulc _____

6. odog _____

7. utoab _____

8. sdlouhtn _____

Spelling Lesson:

As you hear them, write the spelling words for the day in the space provided. Be sure that you correct any words you have spelled incorrectly.

1._____

2._____

3._____

4._____

5._____

6._____

7._____

8._____

9._____

10. _____

11. _____

12. _____

13. _____

14. _____

15. _____

16. _____

17. _____

18. _____

19._____

20. _____

21. _____

22. _____

23. _____

24. _____

25. _____

Using Your Words:

Sound-alike words

wood\would
rout\route\routed

Use a dictionary to find the meanings of these words. Write them in sentences with other words on your spelling list.

1._____

_____

2._____

_____

3._____

_____

4._____

_____

5._____

_____

Day 12

As you hear them, write the spelling words for the day in the space provided. Be sure that you correct any words you have spelled incorrectly.

1._____

2._____

3._____

4._____

5._____

6._____

7._____

8._____

9._____

10. _____

11. _____

12. _____

13. _____

14. _____

15. _____

16. _____

17. _____

18. _____

19._____

20. _____

21. _____

22. _____

23. _____

24. _____

25. _____

Using Your Words:

Sound-alike words

**brood\brewed
mood\mooed**

Use a dictionary to find the meanings of these words. Use them in a sentence with other words on your spelling list.

1._____

_____

2._____

_____

3._____

_____

4._____

_____

Sequential Spelling Level 1 - Student Workbook

Day 13

Spelling Lesson:

As you hear them, write the spelling words for the day in the space provided. Be sure that you correct any words you have spelled incorrectly.

1._____

2._____

3._____

4._____

5._____

6._____

7._____

8._____

9._____

10. _____

11. _____

12. _____

13. _____

14. _____

15. _____

16. _____

17. _____

18. _____

19._____

20. _____

21. _____

22. _____

23. _____

24. _____

25. _____

Using Your Words:

Fill in the blanks with words from today's spelling list.

1. Come in for _____ now.

2. You are doing _____ work.

3. The box is made of _____.

4. Long John Silver had a _____ leg.

5. Why are you in such a bad _____?

6. I will _____ the skies with my e_____.

7. Lindsay st_____ up, th_____ she sat down.

8. My brother is older th_____ my sister.

Day 14

Spelling Lesson:

As you hear them, write the spelling words for the day in the space provided. Be sure that you correct any words you have spelled incorrectly.

1._____

2._____

3._____

4._____

5._____

6._____

7._____

8._____

9._____

10. _____

11. _____

12. _____

13. _____

14. _____

15. _____

16. _____

17. _____

18. _____

19. _____

20. _____

21. _____

22. _____

23. _____

24. _____

25. _____

Using Your Words:

Unscramble these:

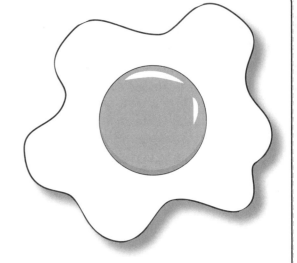

1. ppreu _____

2. pseuprs _____

3. dneoossg _____

4. otosd _____

5. batou _____

6. renasmn _____

7. naht _____

8. tehn _____

Day 15

Spelling Lesson:

As you hear them, write the spelling words for the day in the space provided. Be sure that you correct any words you have spelled incorrectly.

1. _____

2. _____

3. _____

4. _____

5. _____

6. _____

7. _____

8. _____

9. _____

10. _____

11. _____

12. _____

13. _____

14. _____

15. _____

16. _____

17. _____

18. _____

19. _____

20. _____

21. _____

22. _____

23. _____

24. _____

25. _____

Using Your Words:

Sound-alike words

wouldn't\wooden
eye\aye\I
than\then

Use a dictionary to find the meanings of these words. Write them in sentences with other words on your spelling list.

1._____

_____

2._____

_____

3._____

_____

4._____

_____

5._____

_____

6._____

_____

7._____

Day 16

Spelling Lesson:

As you hear them, write the spelling words for the day in the space provided. Be sure that you correct any words you have spelled incorrectly.

1._____

2._____

3._____

4._____

5._____

6._____

7._____

8._____

9._____

10. _____

11. _____

12. _____

13. _____

14. _____

15. _____

16. _____

17. _____

18. _____

19._____

20. _____

21. _____

22. _____

23. _____

24. _____

25. _____

Using Your Words:

Can you find the words?

```
R M H C M S V L P Z C X R L O
D E O U O R E I D O O M E R Q
V T G O S U D W M C B D P J C
L V C G D E L R C R R U P K D
R B N P I Y D D E N O H U V N
S N O U T B C P N X O C S G D
A W Q S C B P V U T D Z C O W
Y M H E R U K I R Y E F H U Q
G W U A X C M F D C D P M T T
K H J G V N I U O W P A A Y N
D O O F C A N T Y E N Y I L D
H V M V S E R Q R N E Q J D L
B S C A D F G L E S C I K B U
N X M Z J H K R W T X A D T O
G O O D N E S S Y M D F C V W
```

Words Used

ayes

bigger

brooded

couldn't

food

goodness

gout

manners

moodier

moody

snout

supper

upper

wouldn't

Day 17

As you hear them, write the spelling words for the day in the space provided. Be sure that you correct any words you have spelled incorrectly.

1. _____

2. _____

3. _____

4. _____

5. _____

6. _____

7. _____

8. _____

9. _____

10. _____

11. _____

12. _____

13. _____

14. _____

15. _____

16. _____

17. _____

18. _____

19. _____

20. _____

21. _____

22. _____

23. _____

24. _____

25. _____

Using Your Words:

Fill in the blanks with words from today's spelling list.

1. I count to _____ before getting angry.

2. You should use a _____ to write a thank you note.

3. What happened _____?

4. It is a _____ fall day.

5. We need to make a _____ for next week.

Day 18

Spelling Lesson:

As you hear them, write the spelling words for the day in the space provided. Be sure that you correct any words you have spelled incorrectly.

1. _____

2. _____

3. _____

4. _____

5. _____

6. _____

7. _____

8. _____

9. _____

10. _____

11. _____

12. _____

13. _____

14. _____

15. _____

16. _____

17. _____

18. _____

19. _____

20. _____

21. _____

22. _____

23. _____

24. _____

25. _____

Using Your Words:

Fill in the blanks with words from today's spelling list.

1. Can you count by _____?

2. I went to the _____ department by mistake.

3. How many _____ were there?

4. My puppy _____ come when I called.

5. I _____ have interrupted you.

6. We were sorry you _____ come with us.

Day 19

Spelling Lesson:

As you hear them, write the spelling words for the day in the space provided. Be sure that you correct any words you have spelled incorrectly.

1. _____

2. _____

3. _____

4. _____

5. _____

6. _____

7. _____

8. _____

9. _____

10. _____

11. _____

12. _____

13. _____

14. _____

15. _____

16. _____

17. _____

18. _____

19. _____

20. _____

21. _____

22. _____

23. _____

24. _____

25. _____

Using Your Words:

Sound-alike words

eyes\ayes

Use a dictionary to find the meanings of these words. Write them in sentences with other words on your spelling list.

1._____

_____

2._____

_____

Sequential Spelling Level 1 - Student Workbook

Day 20

Spelling Lesson:

As you hear them, write the spelling words for the day in the space provided. Be sure that you correct any words you have spelled incorrectly.

1. _____

2. _____

3. _____

4. _____

5. _____

6. _____

7. _____

8. _____

9. _____

10. _____

11. _____

12. _____

13. _____

14. _____

15. _____

16. _____

17. _____

18. _____

19. _____

20. _____

21. _____

22. _____

23. _____

24. _____

25. _____

Using Your Words:

Name as many words as you can that have the following letters (in order) in them.

in

_____

_____

_____

_____

_____

_____

_____

_____

Day 21

Spelling Lesson:

As you hear them, write the spelling words for the day in the space provided. Be sure that you correct any words you have spelled incorrectly.

1. _____

2. _____

3. _____

4. _____

5. _____

6. _____

7. _____

8. _____

9. _____

10. _____

11. _____

12. _____

13. _____

14. _____

15. _____

16. _____

17. _____

18. _____

19. _____

20. _____

21. _____

22. _____

23. _____

24. _____

25. _____

Using Your Words:

Unscramble these:

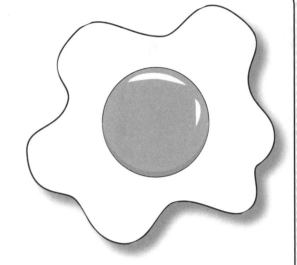

1. arbt _____

2. tpsi _____

3. hooscl _____

4. epon _____

5. olop _____

6. ilt _____

7. loto _____

8. qtui _____

9. tilsp _____

Day 22

As you hear them, write the spelling words for the day in the space provided. Be sure that you correct any words you have spelled incorrectly.

1. _____

2. _____

3. _____

4. _____

5. _____

6. _____

7. _____

8. _____

9. _____

10. _____

11. _____

12. _____

13. _____

14. _____

15. _____

16. _____

17. _____

18. _____

19. _____

20. _____

21. _____

22. _____

23. _____

24. _____

25. _____

Using Your Words:

Sound-alike words

Its\It's

Its is a pronoun which can be used instead of a proper noun. **It's** is a contraction which combines the words **it** and **is**. Show that you understand the difference by writing a sentence using these two words.

1._____

_____

2._____

_____

Sequential Spelling Level 1 - Student Workbook

Day 23

Spelling Lesson:

As you hear them, write the spelling words for the day in the space provided. Be sure that you correct any words you have spelled incorrectly.

1._____

2._____

3._____

4._____

5._____

6._____

7._____

8._____

9._____

10. _____

11. _____

12. _____

13. _____

14. _____

15. _____

16. _____

17. _____

18. _____

19._____

20. _____

21. _____

22. _____

23. _____

24. _____

25. _____

Using Your Words:

Choose five of the words in your spelling list and use each word in a sentence.

1._____

_____

2._____

_____

3._____

_____

4._____

_____

5._____

_____

Day 24

Spelling Lesson:

As you hear them, write the spelling words for the day in the space provided. Be sure that you correct any words you have spelled incorrectly.

1._____

2._____

3._____

4._____

5._____

6._____

7._____

8._____

9._____

10. _____

11. _____

12. _____

13. _____

14. _____

15. _____

16. _____

17. _____

18. _____

19._____

20. _____

21. _____

22. _____

23. _____

24. _____

25. _____

Using Your Words:

Unscramble these:

1. oclhos _____

2. poen _____

3. anht _____

4. nhte _____

5. tqeitru _____

6. ietuq _____

7. cylolo _____

8. tdeflit _____

9. ittigqnu _____

Day 25

Spelling Lesson:

As you hear them, write the spelling words for the day in the space provided. Be sure that you correct any words you have spelled incorrectly.

1. _____

2. _____

3. _____

4. _____

5. _____

6. _____

7. _____

8. _____

9. _____

10. _____

11. _____

12. _____

13. _____

14. _____

15. _____

16. _____

17. _____

18. _____

19. _____

20. _____

21. _____

22. _____

23. _____

24. _____

25. _____

Using Your Words:

Fill in the blanks with words from today's spelling list.

1. I would really like a drink of _____.

2. Would you like to _____ the baby?

3. It gets very _____ in the winter.

4. Did you have a baby _____ when you were little?

5. We need to practice for our sk_____.

6. How many times did you have to sw_____that fly?

7. How _____ do you need to be to herd _____?

8. I would rather have a dog than a _____.

Day 26

As you hear them, write the spelling words for the day in the space provided. Be sure that you correct any words you have spelled incorrectly.

1._____

2._____

3._____

4._____

5._____

6._____

7._____

8._____

9._____

10. _____

11. _____

12. _____

13. _____

14. _____

15. _____

16. _____

17. _____

18. _____

19._____

20. _____

21. _____

22. _____

23. _____

24. _____

25. _____

Using Your Words:

Choose five words from your spelling list and use each of them in a sentence.

1._____

_____

2._____

_____

3._____

_____

4._____

_____

5._____

_____

Spelling Lesson:

As you hear them, write the spelling words for the day in the space provided. Be sure that you correct any words you have spelled incorrectly.

1._____

2._____

3._____

4._____

5._____

6._____

7._____

8._____

9._____

10. _____

11. _____

12. _____

13. _____

14. _____

15. _____

16. _____

17. _____

18. _____

19._____

20. _____

21. _____

22. _____

23. _____

24. _____

25. _____

Using Your Words:

Make as many words as you can from the following word

scattered

_____

_____

_____

_____

_____

_____

_____

_____

_____

_____

Day 28

Spelling Lesson:

As you hear them, write the spelling words for the day in the space provided. Be sure that you correct any words you have spelled incorrectly.

1._____

2._____

3._____

4._____

5._____

6._____

7._____

8._____

9._____

10. _____

11. _____

12. _____

13. _____

14. _____

15. _____

16. _____

17. _____

18. _____

19._____

20. _____

21. _____

22. _____

23. _____

24. _____

25. _____

Using Your Words:

Can you find the words?

```
P  D  M  G  L  N  F  L  B  P  G  S  G  W  U
E  X  E  W  I  O  C  A  N  U  N  N  K  P  L
I  G  T  T  L  X  T  E  T  D  I  E  A  P  A
J  O  R  D  T  T  R  N  Q  R  L  T  F  P  R
V  M  I  O  E  I  S  U  E  T  T  Y  R  F
K  N  T  R  I  E  W  T  L  G  T  I  M  M  D
G  R  I  Y  O  H  A  T  P  M  A  K  F  C  P
G  N  E  D  X  W  H  J  U  C  B  D  B  N  R
G  C  U  T  S  Z  J  O  H  O  S  P  A  T  J
F  L  A  T  T  E  R  Y  L  L  Z  Y  G  N  M
A  Q  V  K  R  A  U  K  U  D  M  M  I  G  Q
S  R  E  D  L  E  W  Q  D  E  I  I  G  Q  A
M  S  S  N  C  R  R  S  L  S  X  N  T  Z  Y
L  E  S  Y  Z  A  F  W  N  T  A  Q  G  H  D
S  E  I  R  E  T  T  A  B  S  D  I  Q  O  V
```

Words Used:

batteries

battering

battling

coldest

doesn't

flattery

folding

holding

kittens

outwitted

spat

swatter

watering

welders

Day 29

Spelling Lesson:

As you hear them, write the spelling words for the day in the space provided. Be sure that you correct any words you have spelled incorrectly.

1._____

2._____

3._____

4._____

5._____

6._____

7._____

8._____

9._____

10. _____

11. _____

12. _____

13. _____

14. _____

15. _____

16. _____

17. _____

18. _____

19._____

20. _____

21. _____

22. _____

23. _____

24. _____

25. _____

Sound-alike words   **told\tolled**   Use a dictionary to find the meanings of these words and then use them in a sentence.

1._____

_____

2._____

_____

Day 30

As you hear them, write the spelling words for the day in the space provided. Be sure that you correct any words you have spelled incorrectly.

1._____

2._____

3._____

4._____

5._____

6._____

7._____

8._____

9._____

10. _____

11. _____

12. _____

13. _____

14. _____

15. _____

16. _____

17. _____

18. _____

19._____

20. _____

21. _____

22. _____

23. _____

24. _____

25. _____

Using Your Words:

Unscramble these:

1. asstterh _____

2. iadtsm _____

3. ctmmois _____

4. septrsta _____

5. hwdtsolih _____

6. ndgelo _____

7. dlreshuos _____

8. buledsor _____

9. egrtlist _____

Day 31

Spelling Lesson:

As you hear them, write the spelling words for the day in the space provided. Be sure that you correct any words you have spelled incorrectly.

1._____

2._____

3._____

4._____

5._____

6._____

7._____

8._____

9._____

10. _____

11. _____

12. _____

13. _____

14. _____

15. _____

16. _____

17. _____

18. _____

19._____

20. _____

21. _____

22. _____

23. _____

24. _____

25. _____

Using Your Words:

Sound-alike words

Fill in the blanks using the correct word: **to\too\two**

It's _____ bad that you _____ girls were late

_____ the movie. Jim and John were _____.

Day 32

As you hear them, write the spelling words for the day in the space provided. Be sure that you correct any words you have spelled incorrectly.

1._____

2._____

3._____

4._____

5._____

6._____

7._____

8._____

9._____

10. _____

11. _____

12. _____

13. _____

14. _____

15. _____

16. _____

17. _____

18. _____

19._____

20. _____

21. _____

22. _____

23. _____

24. _____

25. _____

Using Your Words:

Choose five words from your spelling list and use each of them in a sentence.

1._____

_____

2._____

_____

3._____

_____

4._____

_____

5._____

_____

Sequential Spelling Level 1 - Student Workbook

Day 33

Spelling Lesson:

As you hear them, write the spelling words for the day in the space provided. Be sure that you correct any words you have spelled incorrectly.

1._____

2._____

3._____

4._____

5._____

6._____

7._____

8._____

9._____

10. _____

11. _____

12. _____

13. _____

14. _____

15. _____

16. _____

17. _____

18. _____

19._____

20. _____

21. _____

22. _____

23. _____

24. _____

25. _____

Using Your Words:

Sound-alike words

lot\a lot\allot
bald\bawled\balled

Use a dictionary to find the meanings of these words and then use them in a sentence.

1._____

_____

2._____

_____

3._____

_____

4._____

_____

5._____

_____

6._____

_____

7._____

_____

Day 34

Spelling Lesson:

As you hear them, write the spelling words for the day in the space provided. Be sure that you correct any words you have spelled incorrectly.

1._____

2._____

3._____

4._____

5._____

6._____

7._____

8._____

9._____

10. _____

11. _____

12. _____

13. _____

14. _____

15. _____

16. _____

17. _____

18. _____

19. _____

20. _____

21. _____

22. _____

23. _____

24. _____

25. _____

Using Your Words:

Fill in the blanks with words from today's spelling list.

1. Wasn't that a beautiful s_____?

2. We had a m_____ spring than normal this year.

3. He swung w_____ at the golf ball and missed completely.

4. My dad b_____ bridges. He's an engineer.

5. The doctors c_____ stop the cl_____ from forming.

Day 35

Spelling Lesson:

As you hear them, write the spelling words for the day in the space provided. Be sure that you correct any words you have spelled incorrectly.

1._____

2._____

3._____

4._____

5._____

6._____

7._____

8._____

9._____

10. _____

11. _____

12. _____

13. _____

14. _____

15. _____

16. _____

17. _____

18. _____

19. _____

20. _____

21. _____

22. _____

23. _____

24. _____

25. _____

Using Your Words:

Unscramble these:

1. lnrecidh _____

2. celsdda _____

3. tdeewra _____

4. steupgtni _____

5. tdmisel _____

6. tliub _____

7. ttseedl _____

8. blotetd _____

9. dpostte _____

Day 36

As you hear them, write the spelling words for the day in the space provided. Be sure that you correct any words you have spelled incorrectly.

1._____

2._____

3._____

4._____

5._____

6._____

7._____

8._____

9._____

10. _____

11. _____

12. _____

13. _____

14. _____

15. _____

16. _____

17. _____

18. _____

19._____

20. _____

21. _____

22. _____

23. _____

24. _____

25. _____

Using Your Words:

Sound-alike words

Let is a verb which means to leave. **Let's** is a
contraction which combines the words **let** and **us**.
Fill in the blanks using the correct word.

lets\let's

_____ go shopping after school _____ out.

Day 37

Spelling Lesson:

As you hear them, write the spelling words for the day in the space provided. Be sure that you correct any words you have spelled incorrectly.

1._____

2._____

3._____

4._____

5._____

6._____

7._____

8._____

9._____

10. _____

11. _____

12. _____

13. _____

14. _____

15. _____

16. _____

17. _____

18. _____

19._____

20. _____

21. _____

22. _____

23. _____

24. _____

25. _____

Using Your Words:

Fill in the blanks with words from today's spelling list.

1. Please be q_____. I want to hear the radio.

2. I lost my red g_____. Could you help me find it?

3. A d_____ is often used as a sign of peace.

4. I think that painting is pr_____ than the other one.

5. Abby is a book l_____

6. I know that I s_____, but I won't.

7. She is _____ making too much noise.

8. Could you please untie this k_____?

Day 38

Spelling Lesson:

As you hear them, write the spelling words for the day in the space provided. Be sure that you correct any words you have spelled incorrectly.

1. _____

2. _____

3. _____

4. _____

5. _____

6. _____

7. _____

8. _____

9. _____

10. _____

11. _____

12. _____

13. _____

14. _____

15. _____

16. _____

17. _____

18. _____

19. _____

20. _____

21. _____

22. _____

23. _____

24. _____

25. _____

Using Your Words:

List as many words as you can that have these letters (in order).

ot

_____

_____

_____

_____

_____

_____

_____

_____

_____

Day 39

Spelling Lesson:

As you hear them, write the spelling words for the day in the space provided. Be sure that you correct any words you have spelled incorrectly.

1. _____

2. _____

3. _____

4. _____

5. _____

6. _____

7. _____

8. _____

9. _____

10. _____

11. _____

12. _____

13. _____

14. _____

15. _____

16. _____

17. _____

18. _____

19. _____

20. _____

21. _____

22. _____

23. _____

24. _____

25. _____

Using Your Words:

Choose five words from your spelling list and use each of them in a sentence.

1._____

_____

2._____

_____

3._____

_____

4._____

_____

5._____

_____

Day 40

As you hear them, write the spelling words for the day in the space provided. Be sure that you correct any words you have spelled incorrectly.

1._____

2._____

3._____

4._____

5._____

6._____

7._____

8._____

9._____

10._____

11._____

12._____

13._____

14._____

15._____

16._____

17._____

18._____

19._____

20._____

21._____

22._____

23._____

24._____

25._____

Using Your Words:

Can you find the words?

```
S  S  M  X  L  W  S  C  P  Y  W  E  O  U  S
W  L  X  P  E  R  W  E  U  I  N  X  K  K  H
N  Q  J  K  E  H  R  N  N  D  S  H  Z  N  O
U  Q  S  P  K  M  I  N  V  L  P  T  I  F  V
Z  S  P  F  I  N  E  F  T  U  L  D  I  M  E
B  U  N  T  B  R  V  L  N  O  I  K  G  L  S
S  E  T  I  E  F  S  A  V  W  T  G  L  U  K
C  E  G  J  W  W  U  T  D  J  T  R  L  K  G
D  A  N  I  V  T  I  C  P  E  I  Y  N  G  C
S  Y  I  D  N  F  O  L  D  I  N  G  T  V  N
Q  H  L  X  Q  N  T  M  D  T  G  N  M  B  U
B  A  O  I  L  E  I  S  R  E  T  T  A  L  F
X  L  O  U  S  P  Q  N  T  R  E  E  S  L  T
Y  U  F  P  T  G  T  O  G  R  O  F  T  E  P
L  H  U  R  S  S  J  N  N  D  Q  J  N  Z  Q
```

Words Used

beginning

fit

flat

flatters

folding

fooling

forgot

permitted

planned

shouts

shoves

splitting

suppers

ten

trees

twins

upset

wild

winner

would

Evaluation Test #1

1.   The lady next door just had tw_____.

2.   Let's start at the beg_____.

3.   He planted pine tr_____ in his back yard.

4.   A w_____ never quits.

5.   My friend w_____ always listen to me.

6.   He never just talks. He sh_____.

7.   He eats one lunch and two s_____.

8.   He counted to t_____ on his toes.

9.   She pl_____ a special dinner for him.

10. Please stop f_____ around.

11. The clown fell fl_____ on his face.

12. I was f_____ to be tied.

13. That dress fl_____ her.

14. I have a spl_____ headache.

15. I am forever f_____ laundry.

16. I can't believe he was perm_____ to do that.

17. I hope you're not ups_____ with me.

18. Always be careful around a w_____ animal.

19. It's not funny when someone sh_____ you.

20. I'm sorry I forg_____ to say, "I'm sorry."

Day 41

Spelling Lesson:

As you hear them, write the spelling words for the day in the space provided. Be sure that you correct any words you have spelled incorrectly.

1._____

2._____

3._____

4._____

5._____

6._____

7._____

8._____

9._____

10. _____

11. _____

12. _____

13. _____

14. _____

15. _____

16. _____

17. _____

18. _____

19._____

20. _____

21. _____

22. _____

23. _____

24. _____

25. _____

Using Your Words:

Fill in the blanks with words from today's spelling list.

1. Let me sh_____ you how it's done.

2. B_____ the whistle if you need help.

3. Tom needs to use the _____ to _____ the lawn.

4. That is a large g_____ of orange trees.

5. We had a picnic in the _____.

6. After lunch, Lisa _____ into the lake for a swim.

7. Jason was sl_____ th_____ Andy.

Day 42

Spelling Lesson:

As you hear them, write the spelling words for the day in the space provided. Be sure that you correct any words you have spelled incorrectly.

1._____

2._____

3._____

4._____

5._____

6._____

7._____

8._____

9._____

10. _____

11. _____

12. _____

13. _____

14. _____

15. _____

16. _____

17. _____

18. _____

19._____

20. _____

21. _____

22. _____

23. _____

24. _____

25. _____

Using Your Words:

Look alike words

dove "duv"\dove "d'OH-v"
mow "m'OH"\mow "m'OW"

Use a dictionary to find the definition of *mow "m'OW"*. Then, fill in the blanks with words from today's spelling list.

1. He _____ into the pool.

2. Lisa painted a _____.

3. You can _____ the hay and then put it in the _____.

Day 43

As you hear them, write the spelling words for the day in the space provided. Be sure that you correct any words you have spelled incorrectly.

1._____

2._____

3._____

4._____

5._____

6._____

7._____

8._____

9._____

10. _____

11. _____

12. _____

13. _____

14. _____

15. _____

16. _____

17. _____

18. _____

19. _____

20. _____

21. _____

22. _____

23. _____

24. _____

25. _____

Using Your Words:

List as many words as you can that have the following letters (in order) in them.

ver

_____

_____

_____

_____

_____

_____

_____

_____

_____

Day 44

As you hear them, write the spelling words for the day in the space provided. Be sure that you correct any words you have spelled incorrectly.

1._____

2._____

3._____

4._____

5._____

6._____

7._____

8._____

9._____

10. _____

11. _____

12. _____

13. _____

14. _____

15. _____

16. _____

17. _____

18. _____

19._____

20. _____

21. _____

22. _____

23. _____

24. _____

25. _____

Using Your Words:

Choose five of the words in your spelling list and use each word in a sentence.

1._____

_____

2._____

_____

3._____

_____

4._____

_____

5._____

_____

Day 45

Spelling Lesson:

As you hear them, write the spelling words for the day in the space provided. Be sure that you correct any words you have spelled incorrectly.

1. _____

2. _____

3. _____

4. _____

5. _____

6. _____

7. _____

8. _____

9. _____

10. _____

11. _____

12. _____

13. _____

14. _____

15. _____

16. _____

17. _____

18. _____

19. _____

20. _____

21. _____

22. _____

23. _____

24. _____

25. _____

Using Your Words:

Sound-alike words

rode\road\rowed
toad\towed\toed

Use a dictionary to find the meanings of the words that you don't know. Then, use each word in a sentence.

1._____

_____

2._____

_____

3._____

_____

4._____

_____

5._____

_____

6._____

_____

Day 46

Spelling Lesson:

As you hear them, write the spelling words for the day in the space provided. Be sure that you correct any words you have spelled incorrectly.

1._____

2._____

3._____

4._____

5._____

6._____

7._____

8._____

9._____

10. _____

11. _____

12. _____

13. _____

14. _____

15. _____

16. _____

17. _____

18. _____

19. _____

20. _____

21. _____

22. _____

23. _____

24. _____

25. _____

Using Your Words:

Fill in the blanks with words from today's spelling list.

1. Aren't these lovely _____? Let's get Allison one for her birthday.

2. Jack _____ a horse for the first time yesterday.

3. If we drive, how many _____ do you think it will take us to get to California?

4. You _____ drink so much coffee!

5. Why _____ you finish your work?

6. I _____ poke that hornet's nest. You'll make them angry!

7. Laura _____ know when she will get here.

Day 47

Spelling Lesson:

As you hear them, write the spelling words for the day in the space provided. Be sure that you correct any words you have spelled incorrectly.

1._____

2._____

3._____

4._____

5._____

6._____

7._____

8._____

9._____

10. _____

11. _____

12. _____

13. _____

14. _____

15. _____

16. _____

17. _____

18. _____

19._____

20. _____

21. _____

22. _____

23. _____

24. _____

25. _____

Using Your Words:

Unscramble these:

1. droe _____

2. epxeddol _____

3. iodadlrear _____

4. ydsa _____

5. eanlddou _____

6. pdober _____

7. ogebl _____

8. algolb _____

9. eoadedbrn _____

Day 48

Spelling Lesson:

As you hear them, write the spelling words for the day in the space provided. Be sure that you correct any words you have spelled incorrectly.

1._____

2._____

3._____

4._____

5._____

6._____

7._____

8._____

9._____

10._____

11._____

12._____

13._____

14._____

15._____

16._____

17._____

18._____

19._____

20._____

21._____

22._____

23._____

24._____

25._____

Using Your Words:

Choose five words from your spelling list and use each of them correctly in a sentence.

1._____

_____

2._____

_____

3._____

_____

4._____

_____

5._____

_____

Day 49

As you hear them, write the spelling words for the day in the space provided. Be sure that you correct any words you have spelled incorrectly.

1. _____

2. _____

3. _____

4. _____

5. _____

6. _____

7. _____

8. _____

9. _____

10. _____

11. _____

12. _____

13. _____

14. _____

15. _____

16. _____

17. _____

18. _____

19. _____

20. _____

21. _____

22. _____

23. _____

24. _____

25. _____

Using Your Words:

List as many words as you can that have the following letters (in order) in them.

ay

_____

_____

_____

_____

_____

_____

_____

_____

_____

_____

Day 50

Spelling Lesson:

As you hear them, write the spelling words for the day in the space provided. Be sure that you correct any words you have spelled incorrectly.

1._____

2._____

3._____

4._____

5._____

6._____

7._____

8._____

9._____

10. _____

11. _____

12. _____

13. _____

14. _____

15. _____

16. _____

17. _____

18. _____

19._____

20. _____

21. _____

22. _____

23. _____

24. _____

25. _____

Using Your Words:

Sound-alike words

**prays\preys\praise
grays\greys**

Use a dictionary to find the meanings of the words that you don't know. Then, use each word in a sentence.

I._____

_____

2._____

_____

3._____

_____

4._____

_____

5._____

_____

Day 51

Spelling Lesson:

As you hear them, write the spelling words for the day in the space provided. Be sure that you correct any words you have spelled incorrectly.

1._____

2._____

3._____

4._____

5._____

6._____

7._____

8._____

9._____

10. _____

11. _____

12. _____

13. _____

14. _____

15. _____

16. _____

17. _____

18. _____

19._____

20. _____

21. _____

22. _____

23. _____

24. _____

25. _____

Using Your Words:

Sound-alike words

grayed\grade\greyed

Use a dictionary to find the meanings of the words that you don't know. Then, use each word in a sentence.

1._____

_____

2._____

_____

3._____

_____

Day 52

As you hear them, write the spelling words for the day in the space provided. Be sure that you correct any words you have spelled incorrectly.

1._____

2._____

3._____

4._____

5._____

6._____

7._____

8._____

9._____

10. _____

11. _____

12. _____

13. _____

14. _____

15. _____

16. _____

17. _____

18. _____

19._____

20. _____

21. _____

22. _____

23. _____

24. _____

25. _____

Using Your Words:

Can you  the words?

```
H Y C S E R R F E T D Y T F T
S Z O Y F A C N D O I A A E O
P U E R Y B J G E D S R R R Y
V R N S T O O S Y A P P B C G
G I K D Y S G Y O Y L T F S C
E L R M A N E L N Y A Z M Y R
P R E Y I Y I D N K Y E H T N
A N E Y D R U O A O I J K Z R
T W A I F E A I A N N S D G D
M L K C B O R T N B G B I D K
P N S A B B A N K S G Q B Y X
G N I Y O J N E L H L I Z Q S
T D Z M E Z R A W G B S T D A
Z N I E M H G W M O N D A Y L
N M S I V T I R S S D I R J V
```

Words Used

annoyed

boy

destroy

displaying

enjoying

enjoyment

gray

grey

Monday

playing

pray

prey

rays

Sunday

they

today

toy

Day 53

As you hear them, write the spelling words for the day in the space provided. Be sure that you correct any words you have spelled incorrectly.

1._____

2._____

3._____

4._____

5._____

6._____

7._____

8._____

9._____

10. _____

11. _____

12. _____

13. _____

14. _____

15. _____

16. _____

17. _____

18. _____

19._____

20. _____

21. _____

22. _____

23. _____

24. _____

25. _____

Using Your Words:

Sound-alike words

loan\lone; moan\mown
thrown\throne; shown\shone
grown\groan

Find the meanings of the words that you don't know. Then, use each word in a sentence.

1._____

_____

2._____

_____

3._____

_____

4._____

_____

5._____

_____

6._____

_____

7._____

_____

8._____

_____

9._____

_____

10._____

_____

Sequential Spelling Level 1 - Student Workbook

Day 54

As you hear them, write the spelling words for the day in the space provided. Be sure that you correct any words you have spelled incorrectly.

1._____

2._____

3._____

4._____

5._____

6._____

7._____

8._____

9._____

10. _____

11. _____

12. _____

13._____

14. _____

15. _____

16. _____

17. _____

18. _____

19._____

20. _____

21. _____

22. _____

23. _____

24. _____

25. _____

Using Your Words:

Fill in the blanks with words from today's spelling list.

1. While we were _____, Tim took care of our pets.

2. We will _____ wonder what happened to her.

3. I should have _____ that math fact!

4. Can you smell the new _____ grass?

5. Those _____ tomatoes are delicious!

6. The bank made several _____ to them.

7. I wonder if the _____ will return to claim their pets.

8. Dad _____ that _____ know best.

Spelling Lesson:

As you hear them, write the spelling words for the day in the space provided. Be sure that you correct any words you have spelled incorrectly.

1. _____

2. _____

3. _____

4. _____

5. _____

6. _____

7. _____

8. _____

9. _____

10. _____

11. _____

12. _____

13. _____

14. _____

15. _____

16. _____

17. _____

18. _____

19. _____

20. _____

21. _____

22. _____

23. _____

24. _____

25. _____

Using Your Words:

Look alike words

does "duz"
does "d'OH-z"

Write a sentence using each of these words correctly.
Be sure to include the word "doesn't" as well as does.

_____

_____

_____

_____

_____

_____

_____

_____

_____

_____

Sequential Spelling Level 1 - Student Workbook

Spelling Lesson:

As you hear them, write the spelling words for the day in the space provided. Be sure that you correct any words you have spelled incorrectly.

1._____

2._____

3._____

4._____

5._____

6._____

7._____

8._____

9._____

10. _____

11. _____

12. _____

13. _____

14. _____

15. _____

16. _____

17. _____

18. _____

19._____

20. _____

21. _____

22. _____

23. _____

24. _____

25. _____

Using Your Words:

Choose five words from your spelling list and use each of them correctly in a sentence.

1._____

_____

2._____

_____

3._____

_____

4._____

_____

5._____

_____

Day 57

Spelling Lesson:

As you hear them, write the spelling words for the day in the space provided. Be sure that you correct any words you have spelled incorrectly.

1._____

2._____

3._____

4._____

5._____

6._____

7._____

8._____

9._____

10. _____

11. _____

12. _____

13. _____

14. _____

15. _____

16. _____

17. _____

18. _____

19._____

20. _____

21. _____

22. _____

23. _____

24. _____

25. _____

117

Using Your Words:

List as many words as you can which have the following letters (in order) in them.

ar

_____

_____

_____

_____

_____

_____

_____

_____

_____

_____

Day 58

Spelling Lesson:

As you hear them, write the spelling words for the day in the space provided. Be sure that you correct any words you have spelled incorrectly.

1. _____

2. _____

3. _____

4. _____

5. _____

6. _____

7. _____

8. _____

9. _____

10. _____

11. _____

12. _____

13. _____

14. _____

15. _____

16. _____

17. _____

18. _____

19. _____

20. _____

21. _____

22. _____

23. _____

24. _____

25. _____

Using Your Words:

Sound-alike words

> time\thyme
> march\March
> marches\March's

Find the meanings of the words that you don't know. Then, use each word in a sentence.

1. _____

_____

2. _____

_____

3. _____

_____

4. _____

_____

5. _____

_____

6. _____

_____

Day 59

Spelling Lesson:

As you hear them, write the spelling words for the day in the space provided. Be sure that you correct any words you have spelled incorrectly.

1._____

2._____

3._____

4._____

5._____

6._____

7._____

8._____

9._____

10. _____

11. _____

12. _____

13. _____

14. _____

15. _____

16. _____

17. _____

18. _____

19._____

20. _____

21. _____

22. _____

23. _____

24. _____

25. _____

Using Your Words:

Fill in the blanks with words from today's spelling list.

1. Is your house very _____?

2. The door was _____.

3. Where _____ you? I waited for half an hour before I left.

4. _____ she have a hat? It's cold!

5. Did you get yellow _____ at the soccer game?

6. The best pie crusts are made with _____.

7. That was the _____ I've ever studied.

Day 60

Spelling Lesson:

As you hear them, write the spelling words for the day in the space provided. Be sure that you correct any words you have spelled incorrectly.

1._____

2._____

3._____

4._____

5._____

6._____

7._____

8._____

9._____

10. _____

11. _____

12. _____

13. _____

14. _____

15. _____

16. _____

17. _____

18. _____

19._____

20. _____

21. _____

22. _____

23. _____

24. _____

25. _____

Using Your Words:

Unscramble these:

1. fara _____

2. camrh _____

3. anrirgb _____

4. meit _____

5. arts _____

6. mier _____

7. eyhrm _____

8. mtnigi _____

9. unrfgagesdia _____

Day 61

Spelling Lesson:

As you hear them, write the spelling words for the day in the space provided. Be sure that you correct any words you have spelled incorrectly.

1._____

2._____

3._____

4._____

5._____

6._____

7._____

8._____

9._____

10. _____

11. _____

12. _____

13. _____

14. _____

15. _____

16. _____

17. _____

18. _____

19._____

20. _____

21. _____

22. _____

23. _____

24. _____

25. _____

Using Your Words:

Fill in the blanks with words from today's spelling list.

1. Let's go _____. I'm ready for bed.

2. _____ is the capital of Italy.

3. That is a cute garden _____.

4. Do you use _____ to wash your hands?

5. Would you please _____ still?

6. What is a _____ number?

7. Did you _____ the directions?

Day 62

Spelling Lesson:

As you hear them, write the spelling words for the day in the space provided. Be sure that you correct any words you have spelled incorrectly.

1._____

2._____

3._____

4._____

5._____

6._____

7._____

8._____

9._____

10. _____

11. _____

12. _____

13. _____

14. _____

15. _____

16. _____

17. _____

18. _____

19._____

20. _____

21. _____

22. _____

23. _____

24. _____

25. _____

Using Your Words:

Sound-alike words

Rome\roam
gnome\Nome

Find the meanings of the words that you don't know. Then, use each word in a sentence.

1._____

_____

2._____

_____

3._____

_____

4._____

_____

Day 63

Spelling Lesson:

As you hear them, write the spelling words for the day in the space provided. Be sure that you correct any words you have spelled incorrectly.

1._____

2._____

3._____

4._____

5._____

6._____

7._____

8._____

9._____

10. _____

11. _____

12. _____

13. _____

14. _____

15. _____

16. _____

17. _____

18. _____

19._____

20. _____

21. _____

22. _____

23. _____

24. _____

25. _____

Using Your Words:

Choose five words from today's spelling list and use each in a sentence.

1._____

_____

2._____

_____

3._____

_____

4._____

_____

5._____

_____

Day 64

Spelling Lesson:

As you hear them, write the spelling words for the day in the space provided. Be sure that you correct any words you have spelled incorrectly.

1._____

2._____

3._____

4._____

5._____

6._____

7._____

8._____

9._____

10. _____

11. _____

12. _____

13. _____

14. _____

15. _____

16. _____

17. _____

18. _____

19._____

20. _____

21. _____

22. _____

23. _____

24. _____

25. _____

Using Your Words:

Can You find the Words?

```
G N I O G I L F X G N P O G D
S T A O C R E V O N Q R N C W
C I Z O F I E U F I J I G J P
H H M V X O I O I T T M Q F R
D X I N A E W O M A L I H O X
B N Z M D I N R O O G N R O I
B I A T I H U L Z L V G W U Z
Y F Y H O N F I Y B N F D C Q
S M R M R K G F O A M I N G A
P T I Q R E W J S T F Z I A K
Q N A V F W D N V K X W S G B
G J M O O O T N V A W W N G V
P W X S M I S N U U R I Z X G
W O P Y X L D C H X C J E I A
O J B H P W T M E W Y T F O R
```

Words Used

bloating

chiming

floating

foaming

going

homing

moats

overcoats

priming

underhand

Day 65

Spelling Lesson:

As you hear them, write the spelling words for the day in the space provided. Be sure that you correct any words you have spelled incorrectly.

1._____

2._____

3._____

4._____

5._____

6._____

7._____

8._____

9._____

10. _____

11. _____

12. _____

13. _____

14. _____

15. _____

16. _____

17. _____

18. _____

19._____

20. _____

21. _____

22. _____

23. _____

24. _____

25. _____

Using Your Words:

List as many words as you can that have the following letters (in order) in them.

end

Day 66

As you hear them, write the spelling words for the day in the space provided. Be sure that you correct any words you have spelled incorrectly.

1._____

2._____

3._____

4._____

5._____

6._____

7._____

8._____

9._____

10. _____

11. _____

12. _____

13. _____

14. _____

15. _____

16. _____

17. _____

18. _____

19._____

20. _____

21. _____

22. _____

23. _____

24. _____

25. _____

Using Your Words:

Sound-alike words

lends\lens; bands\bans band\banned

Find the meanings of the words that you don't know. Then, use each word in a sentence.

1._____

_____

2._____

_____

3._____

_____

4._____

_____

5._____

_____

6._____

_____

Day 67

As you hear them, write the spelling words for the day in the space provided. Be sure that you correct any words you have spelled incorrectly.

1._____

2._____

3._____

4._____

5._____

6._____

7._____

8._____

9._____

10. _____

11. _____

12. _____

13. _____

14. _____

15. _____

16. _____

17. _____

18. _____

19._____

20. _____

21. _____

22. _____

23. _____

24. _____

25. _____

Using Your Words:

Unscramble these:

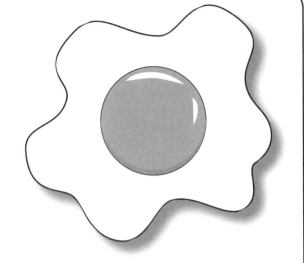

1. dndee _____

2. betn _____

3. ebndedl _____

4. gepbapi _____

5. bddean _____

6. tmeid _____

7. eedtmbi _____

8. cnimalir _____

9. dbnrdeeife _____

Day 68

Spelling Lesson:

As you hear them, write the spelling words for the day in the space provided. Be sure that you correct any words you have spelled incorrectly.

1._____

2._____

3._____

4._____

5._____

6._____

7._____

8._____

9._____

10. _____

11. _____

12. _____

13. _____

14. _____

15. _____

16. _____

17. _____

18. _____

19._____

20. _____

21. _____

22. _____

23. _____

24. _____

25. _____

Using Your Words:

Fill in the blanks with words from today's spelling list.

1. In the _____, let's make lunch.

2. _____ are judged for their _____.

3. Sometimes, a small town is _____ than a big city.

4. The airport is _____ all flights due to the snow.

5. In Scotland, the music of _____ is heard frequently.

6. Wheat and oats _____ in the fields.

7. What's he _____ about now?

Day 69

Spelling Lesson:

As you hear them, write the spelling words for the day in the space provided. Be sure that you correct any words you have spelled incorrectly.

1._____

2._____

3._____

4._____

5._____

6._____

7._____

8._____

9._____

10. _____

11. _____

12. _____

13. _____

14. _____

15. _____

16. _____

17. _____

18. _____

19. _____

20. _____

21. _____

22. _____

23. _____

24. _____

25. _____

Using Your Words:

Use a dictionary to find the meanings of the following words and use them in a sentence.

1. commend _____

_____

2. recommend _____

_____

3. tripe _____

_____

4. snipe _____

_____

5. sniper _____

_____

6. bland _____

_____

Day 70

As you hear them, write the spelling words for the day in the space provided. Be sure that you correct any words you have spelled incorrectly.

1._____

2._____

3._____

4._____

5._____

6._____

7._____

8._____

9._____

10. _____

11. _____

12. _____

13. _____

14. _____

15. _____

16. _____

17. _____

18. _____

19._____

20. _____

21. _____

22. _____

23. _____

24. _____

25. _____

Using Your Words:

Fill in the blanks with words from today's spelling list.

1. A tailor _____ men's clothes.

2. _____ he look handsome in that tuxedo?

3. He _____ come when he was called.

4. I'm sorry if that _____ you.

5. My mother _____ me candy for my birthday.

6. A snow shovel is _____ to have in winter.

Day 71

As you hear them, write the spelling words for the day in the space provided. Be sure that you correct any words you have spelled incorrectly.

1._____

2._____

3._____

4._____

5._____

6._____

7._____

8._____

9._____

10. _____

11. _____

12. _____

13. _____

14. _____

15. _____

16. _____

17. _____

18. _____

19._____

20. _____

21. _____

22. _____

23. _____

24. _____

25. _____

Using Your Words:

Sound-alike words

were\we're

Find the definitions of these words and use them correctly in a sentence.

1._____

_____

2._____

_____

Day 72

As you hear them, write the spelling words for the day in the space provided. Be sure that you correct any words you have spelled incorrectly.

1._____

2._____

3._____

4._____

5._____

6._____

7._____

8._____

9._____

10. _____

11. _____

12. _____

13. _____

14. _____

15. _____

16. _____

17. _____

18. _____

19._____

20. _____

21. _____

22. _____

23. _____

24. _____

25. _____

Using Your Words:

Choose five words from today's spelling list and use each in a sentence.

1._____

_____

2._____

_____

3._____

_____

4._____

_____

5._____

_____

Day 73

Spelling Lesson:

As you hear them, write the spelling words for the day in the space provided. Be sure that you correct any words you have spelled incorrectly.

1._____

2._____

3._____

4._____

5._____

6._____

7._____

8._____

9._____

10. _____

11. _____

12. _____

13. _____

14. _____

15. _____

16. _____

17. _____

18. _____

19._____

20. _____

21. _____

22. _____

23. _____

24. _____

25. _____

Using Your Words:

Sound-alike words

bite\byte
right\rite\write
sight\site\cite

Find the meanings of the words that you don't know. Then, use each word I in a sentence.

1._____

_____

2._____

_____

3._____

_____

4._____

_____

5._____

_____

6._____

_____

7._____

_____

8._____

_____

Spelling Lesson:

As you hear them, write the spelling words for the day in the space provided. Be sure that you correct any words you have spelled incorrectly.

1._____

2._____

3._____

4._____

5._____

6._____

7._____

8._____

9._____

10. _____

11. _____

12. _____

13. _____

14. _____

15. _____

16. _____

17. _____

18. _____

19._____

20. _____

21. _____

22. _____

23. _____

24. _____

25. _____

Using Your Words:

List as many words as you can which have the following letters (in order) in them.

ight

Day 75

As you hear them, write the spelling words for the day in the space provided. Be sure that you correct any words you have spelled incorrectly.

1._____

2._____

3._____

4._____

5._____

6._____

7._____

8._____

9._____

10. _____

11. _____

12. _____

13. _____

14. _____

15. _____

16. _____

17. _____

18. _____

19._____

20. _____

21. _____

22. _____

23. _____

24. _____

25. _____

Using Your Words:

Fill in the blanks with words from today's spelling list.

1. I _____ down too hard and broke my tooth.

2. She _____ her a recommendation for college.

3. Can you read what you've _____?

4. Is that a dust _____?

5. Alan _____ need to leave earlier than usual.

6. Ellen _____ her research paper.

7. Nancy and Connie _____ the meeting.

8. Rob _____ that as one of the reasons he's leaving.

Day 76

As you hear them, write the spelling words for the day in the space provided. Be sure that you correct any words you have spelled incorrectly.

1._____

2._____

3._____

4._____

5._____

6._____

7._____

8._____

9._____

10. _____

11. _____

12. _____

13. _____

14. _____

15. _____

16. _____

17. _____

18. _____

19._____

20. _____

21. _____

22. _____

23. _____

24. _____

25. _____

Using Your Words:

Unscramble these:

1. inrdef   _____

2. niwttre   _____

3. ietwr   _____

4. ktei   _____

5. siet   _____

6. hstgi   _____

7. lgith   _____

8. rdesepsun _____

9. ctdeire   _____

Day 77

Spelling Lesson:

As you hear them, write the spelling words for the day in the space provided. Be sure that you correct any words you have spelled incorrectly.

1._____

2._____

3._____

4._____

5._____

6._____

7._____

8._____

9._____

10. _____

11. _____

12. _____

13. _____

14. _____

15. _____

16. _____

17. _____

18. _____

19._____

20. _____

21. _____

22. _____

23. _____

24. _____

25. _____

Using Your Words:

Choose five words from today's spelling list and use each in a sentence.

1._____

_____

2._____

_____

3._____

_____

4._____

_____

5._____

_____

Spelling Lesson:

As you hear them, write the spelling words for the day in the space provided. Be sure that you correct any words you have spelled incorrectly.

1._____

2._____

3._____

4._____

5._____

6._____

7._____

8._____

9._____

10. _____

11. _____

12. _____

13. _____

14. _____

15. _____

16. _____

17. _____

18. _____

19._____

20. _____

21. _____

22. _____

23. _____

24. _____

25. _____

Using Your Words:

Sound-alike words

night\knight

Find the definitions of these words and use them correctly in a sentence.

1._____

_____

2._____

_____

Day 79

As you hear them, write the spelling words for the day in the space provided. Be sure that you correct any words you have spelled incorrectly.

1._____

2._____

3._____

4._____

5._____

6._____

7._____

8._____

9._____

10. _____

11. _____

12. _____

13. _____

14. _____

15. _____

16. _____

17. _____

18. _____

19._____

20. _____

21. _____

22. _____

23. _____

24. _____

25. _____

Using Your Words:

Fill in the blanks with words from today's spelling list.

1. Where _____ you this morning? We missed you!

2. I'm not _____ done with this job.

3. _____ Jack know where we are?

4. You really _____ my day with those flowers you sent.

5. _____ sometimes wore suits of armor.

Day 80

Spelling Lesson:

As you hear them, write the spelling words for the day in the space provided. Be sure that you correct any words you have spelled incorrectly.

1. _____

2. _____

3. _____

4. _____

5. _____

6. _____

7. _____

8. _____

9. _____

10. _____

11. _____

12. _____

13. _____

14. _____

15. _____

16. _____

17. _____

18. _____

19. _____

20. _____

21. _____

22. _____

23. _____

24. _____

25. _____

Using Your Words

Can You find The Words?

L	H	D	R	L	Q	R	H	E	U	E	G	L	L	I
W	W	L	E	O	U	I	M	N	S	R	N	G	K	E
Y	G	P	S	N	E	G	M	I	O	E	I	V	Y	X
E	M	V	E	E	E	H	W	P	J	W	N	C	R	T
M	E	V	G	W	O	T	A	F	L	H	T	R	N	W
P	A	R	Q	E	K	D	H	V	N	B	H	S	G	M
S	A	F	E	U	T	B	L	G	Y	X	G	N	Y	B
E	Y	Z	C	H	I	R	Y	N	I	E	I	M	W	I
C	K	C	G	V	E	T	I	W	F	R	L	N	H	Z
W	H	I	T	E	N	G	E	V	A	R	B	Z	G	Q
E	N	H	W	I	H	P	R	V	E	I	E	M	E	Z
K	N	X	Y	T	N	H	N	N	V	O	M	J	I	M
U	Q	E	E	G	Y	K	B	Y	C	O	F	X	B	H
E	X	O	M	U	S	J	N	M	L	H	V	P	C	F
N	J	Q	M	N	N	Z	H	U	T	L	U	W	A	K

Words Used

brave

brightened

does

knight

lightning

night

quite

right

safe

save

were

white

Evaluation Test #2

1. A bully is always sh_____ others around.

2. I like to play "Sh_____ and Tell." Don't you?

3. We dr_____ there, but it took us four hours.

4. He's just bl_____ off steam.

5. We got him a bath r_____ for his birthday.

6. She really expl_____.

7. I really enj_____ listening to good music.

8. The airplane was del_____ by fog.

9. I l_____ Pat five dollars a week ago.

10. We got s_____ wet.

11. Cr_____ doesn't pay.

12. They left the dump ungu_____.

13. Who is in the st_____ role?

14. Do you like to watch soldiers m_____?

15. There's no place like h_____.

16. We need a new bar of s_____.

17. We came to an underst_____.

18. It all dep_____ upon your point of view.

19. They dem_____ equal rights.

20. The movie was very exc_____.

Day 81

Spelling Lesson:

As you hear them, write the spelling words for the day in the space provided. Be sure that you correct any words you have spelled incorrectly.

1._____

2._____

3._____

4._____

5._____

6._____

7._____

8._____

9._____

10._____

11._____

12._____

13._____

14._____

15._____

16._____

17._____

18._____

19._____

20._____

21._____

22._____

23._____

24._____

25._____

Using Your Words:

Fill in the blanks with words from today's spelling list.

1. I'll need to see if my mom will _____ of this idea.

2. She _____ me a pretty red sweater for my birthday.

3. I will ask the jeweler to _____ the ring.

4. Don't forget to _____ goodbye.

5. Do you _____ the plane tickets?

6. Could you please help me _____ this chair?

7. We need to _____ by 5:00 to get there on time.

8. Do you hear rain on the _____?

Day 82

As you hear them, write the spelling words for the day in the space provided. Be sure that you correct any words you have spelled incorrectly.

1._____

2._____

3._____

4._____

5._____

6._____

7._____

8._____

9._____

10. _____

11. _____

12. _____

13. _____

14. _____

15. _____

16. _____

17. _____

18. _____

19._____

20. _____

21. _____

22. _____

23. _____

24. _____

25. _____

Using Your Words:

Leaf and *Leave* can have different meanings depending on how they are used. Write four sentences using the singular and plural forms correctly.

1._____

_____

2._____

_____

3._____

_____

4._____

_____

Day 83

Spelling Lesson:

As you hear them, write the spelling words for the day in the space provided. Be sure that you correct any words you have spelled incorrectly.

1._____

2._____

3._____

4._____

5._____

6._____

7._____

8._____

9._____

10. _____

11. _____

12. _____

13. _____

14. _____

15. _____

16. _____

17. _____

18. _____

19._____

20. _____

21. _____

22. _____

23. _____

24. _____

25. _____

Using Your Words:

Choose five words from today's spelling list and use each in a sentence.

1._____

_____

2._____

_____

3._____

_____

4._____

_____

5._____

_____

Sequential Spelling Level 1 - Student Workbook

Day 84

As you hear them, write the spelling words for the day in the space provided. Be sure that you correct any words you have spelled incorrectly.

1._____

2._____

3._____

4._____

5._____

6._____

7._____

8._____

9._____

10. _____

11. _____

12. _____

13. _____

14. _____

15. _____

16. _____

17. _____

18. _____

19._____

20. _____

21. _____

22. _____

23. _____

24. _____

25. _____

Using Your Words:

Unscramble these:

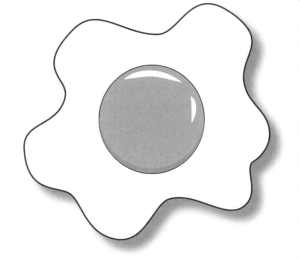

1. smiavhebe _____

2. oeafvgr _____

3. olorofofp _____

4. easvel _____

5. rreabyv _____

6. aigergvnn _____

7. aroepdvp _____

8. ormev _____

9. ovimse _____

Day 85

As you hear them, write the spelling words for the day in the space provided. Be sure that you correct any words you have spelled incorrectly.

1._____

2._____

3._____

4._____

5._____

6._____

7._____

8._____

9._____

10. _____

11. _____

12. _____

13. _____

14. _____

15. _____

16. _____

17. _____

18. _____

19._____

20. _____

21. _____

22. _____

23. _____

24. _____

25. _____

Using Your Words:

List as many words as you can which have the following letters (in order) in them.

all

_____

_____

_____

_____

_____

_____

_____

_____

_____

_____

Sequential Spelling Level 1 - Student Workbook

Day 86

Spelling Lesson:

As you hear them, write the spelling words for the day in the space provided. Be sure that you correct any words you have spelled incorrectly.

1. _____

2. _____

3. _____

4. _____

5. _____

6. _____

7. _____

8. _____

9. _____

10. _____

11. _____

12. _____

13. _____

14. _____

15. _____

16. _____

17. _____

18. _____

19. _____

20. _____

21. _____

22. _____

23. _____

24. _____

25. _____

Using Your Words:

Fill in the blanks with words from today's spelling list.

1. How _____ do you get a cold?

2. The snow is falling so _____ into such pretty _____.

3. What caused the _____ between them?

4. We _____ going to give you the _____ just yet.

5. How many loan _____ do you have to go?

6. _____ she work several _____ this week?

7. Jack painted the _____ of his bedroom yellow.

Day 87

Spelling Lesson:

As you hear them, write the spelling words for the day in the space provided. Be sure that you correct any words you have spelled incorrectly.

1._____

2._____

3._____

4._____

5._____

6._____

7._____

8._____

9._____

10. _____

11. _____

12. _____

13. _____

14. _____

15. _____

16. _____

17. _____

18. _____

19._____

20. _____

21. _____

22. _____

23. _____

24. _____

25. _____

Using Your Words:

Contractions

A **contraction** is a shortened form of one or two words – one of which is usually a verb. Tell which two words the following contractions contain.

isn't _____

wasn't _____

doesn't _____

weren't _____

shouldn't _____

Sequential Spelling Level 1 - Student Workbook

Day 88

As you hear them, write the spelling words for the day in the space provided. Be sure that you correct any words you have spelled incorrectly.

1._____

2._____

3._____

4._____

5._____

6._____

7._____

8._____

9._____

10. _____

11. _____

12. _____

13. _____

14. _____

15. _____

16. _____

17. _____

18. _____

19._____

20. _____

21. _____

22. _____

23. _____

24. _____

25. _____

Using Your Words:

Choose five words from today's spelling list and use each in a sentence.

1._____

_____

2._____

_____

3._____

_____

4._____

_____

5._____

_____

Day 89

Spelling Lesson:

As you hear them, write the spelling words for the day in the space provided. Be sure that you correct any words you have spelled incorrectly.

1._____

2._____

3._____

4._____

5._____

6._____

7._____

8._____

9._____

10. _____

11. _____

12. _____

13. _____

14. _____

15. _____

16. _____

17. _____

18. _____

19._____

20. _____

21. _____

22. _____

23. _____

24. _____

25. _____

Using Your Words:

List as many words as you can that have the following letters (in order) in them.

ig

_____

_____

_____

_____

_____

_____

_____

_____

_____

_____

Day 90

As you hear them, write the spelling words for the day in the space provided. Be sure that you correct any words you have spelled incorrectly.

1._____

2._____

3._____

4._____

5._____

6._____

7._____

8._____

9._____

10. _____

11. _____

12. _____

13. _____

14. _____

15. _____

16. _____

17. _____

18. _____

19._____

20. _____

21. _____

22. _____

23. _____

24. _____

25. _____

Using Your Words:

Make a rhyme or silly story using five of today's spelling words.

_____

_____

_____

_____

_____

_____

_____

_____

_____

_____

Day 91

Spelling Lesson:

As you hear them, write the spelling words for the day in the space provided. Be sure that you correct any words you have spelled incorrectly.

1. _____

2. _____

3. _____

4. _____

5. _____

6. _____

7. _____

8. _____

9. _____

10. _____

11. _____

12. _____

13. _____

14. _____

15. _____

16. _____

17. _____

18. _____

19. _____

20. _____

21. _____

22. _____

23. _____

24. _____

25. _____

Using Your Words:

Fill in the blanks with words from today's spelling list.

1. Jack stepped on a _____ and it snapped loudly.

2. _____ Lizzie joined me, I was by _____.

3. My puppy _____ out of his leash and ran away.

4. The lightning strike _____ the fire.

5. Sharon and Linda _____ at the joke.

6. _____ she need any help?

7. What _____ you doing?

8. My piece of cake _____ the _____.

Day 92

Spelling Lesson:

As you hear them, write the spelling words for the day in the space provided. Be sure that you correct any words you have spelled incorrectly.

1._____

2._____

3._____

4._____

5._____

6._____

7._____

8._____

9._____

10._____

11._____

12._____

13._____

14._____

15._____

16._____

17._____

18._____

19._____

20._____

21._____

22._____

23._____

24._____

25._____

Using Your Words

Can you find the Words?

```
O Z V B F P P G B Q F F M U D
P C O S F O Z N Y J I L I F V
D K G J T Y K I O R L E H G P
N P M N N I S H F K L S U A S
A Y P R B Y L C L Z I Y B Q R
G N I L L I F L U F N M P K A
S E V L A H I I I F G D T N L
I E E R W M N F G N I M E I K
F G V W E R E N R G G M T G Z
E L E L P G I G G L I N G M E
E C E V E L Y E U U U P F E B
O N F S L S R Q E V A B T T I
B V L I T S R Y P L F D U A G
R G P M O I B U T J A R A J B
S S S D F U Y J O E H Q X W Q
```

Words Used

diggers

figs

filching

filling

fulfilling

giggling

halves

itself

myself

ourselves

spilling

stilling

until

were

Day 93

Spelling Lesson:

As you hear them, write the spelling words for the day in the space provided. Be sure that you correct any words you have spelled incorrectly.

1._____

2._____

3._____

4._____

5._____

6._____

7._____

8._____

9._____

10. _____

11. _____

12. _____

13. _____

14. _____

15. _____

16. _____

17. _____

18. _____

19._____

20. _____

21. _____

22. _____

23. _____

24. _____

25. _____

Using Your Words:

Fill in the blanks with words from today's spelling list.

1. Did _____ pay the _____?

2. _____ that _____ Mr. Smith?

3. What a _____ it was to see that hockey game!

4. What's the name of your _____?

5. _____ is a problem in many cities.

6. _____ you please cut that in _____?

Spelling Lesson:

As you hear them, write the spelling words for the day in the space provided. Be sure that you correct any words you have spelled incorrectly.

1._____

2._____

3._____

4._____

5._____

6._____

7._____

8._____

9._____

10. _____

11. _____

12. _____

13. _____

14. _____

15. _____

16. _____

17. _____

18. _____

19._____

20. _____

21. _____

22. _____

23. _____

24. _____

25. _____

Using Your Words:

List as many words as you can that have the following letters (in order) in them.

ill

_____

_____

_____

_____

_____

_____

_____

_____

_____

_____

Day 95

Spelling Lesson:

As you hear them, write the spelling words for the day in the space provided. Be sure that you correct any words you have spelled incorrectly.

1._____

2._____

3._____

4._____

5._____

6._____

7._____

8._____

9._____

10. _____

11. _____

12. _____

13. _____

14. _____

15. _____

16. _____

17. _____

18. _____

19._____

20. _____

21. _____

22. _____

23. _____

24. _____

25. _____

Using Your Words:

Sound-alike words

billed\build

Find the definitions of these words and use them correctly in a sentence.

_____

_____

_____

_____

_____

_____

_____

_____

_____

_____

Day 96

Spelling Lesson:

As you hear them, write the spelling words for the day in the space provided. Be sure that you correct any words you have spelled incorrectly.

1._____

2._____

3._____

4._____

5._____

6._____

7._____

8._____

9._____

10. _____

11. _____

12. _____

13. _____

14. _____

15. _____

16. _____

17. _____

18. _____

19._____

20. _____

21. _____

22. _____

23. _____

24. _____

25. _____

Using Your Words:

Make a rhyme or silly story using five of today's spelling words.

_____

_____

_____

_____

_____

_____

_____

_____

_____

_____

Spelling Lesson:

As you hear them, write the spelling words for the day in the space provided. Be sure that you correct any words you have spelled incorrectly.

1._____

2._____

3._____

4._____

5._____

6._____

7._____

8._____

9._____

10. _____

11. _____

12. _____

13. _____

14. _____

15. _____

16. _____

17. _____

18. _____

19._____

20. _____

21. _____

22. _____

23. _____

24. _____

25. _____

Using Your Words:

Unscramble these:

1. glir _____

2. leam _____

3. elfe _____

4. eehl _____

5. elpe _____

6. arel _____

7. hael _____

8. celaer _____

9. eiarsl _____

Day 98

Spelling Lesson:

As you hear them, write the spelling words for the day in the space provided. Be sure that you correct any words you have spelled incorrectly.

1._____

2._____

3._____

4._____

5._____

6._____

7._____

8._____

9._____

10. _____

11. _____

12. _____

13. _____

14. _____

15. _____

16. _____

17. _____

18. _____

19._____

20. _____

21. _____

22. _____

23. _____

24. _____

25. _____

Using Your Words:

Sound-alike words

heel\heal; peel\peal
reel\real; steal\steel
cereal\serial

Find the definitions of each of these sets of words and then use them in a sentence.

1._____

_____

2._____

_____

3._____

_____

4._____

_____

5._____

_____

6._____

_____

7._____

_____

8._____

_____

9._____

_____

10._____

Spelling Lesson:

As you hear them, write the spelling words for the day in the space provided. Be sure that you correct any words you have spelled incorrectly.

1._____

2._____

3._____

4._____

5._____

6._____

7._____

8._____

9._____

10. _____

11. _____

12. _____

13. _____

14. _____

15. _____

16. _____

17. _____

18. _____

19._____

20. _____

21. _____

22. _____

23. _____

24. _____

25. _____

Using Your Words:

Can you find the words?

```
D  L  A  S  T  E  L  H  L  Z  B  P  U  Y  Z
Y  P  R  L  R  A  I  S  T  L  A  E  D  R  P
S  V  E  I  I  E  T  D  E  L  A  E  P  P  A
E  F  G  R  G  E  L  R  P  E  A  L  E  D  Y
O  W  E  F  E  W  E  A  E  A  F  E  Q  Y  E
D  S  Y  L  H  V  M  W  E  X  M  R  A  F  E
A  V  Z  T  E  W  S  B  S  S  H  F  B  E  W
U  M  W  A  H  J  I  P  I  E  T  E  K  I  S
L  I  L  J  J  Q  Q  B  T  K  A  V  E  Q  F
E  E  E  S  Z  K  F  R  D  S  L  L  B  C  A
D  V  U  C  E  P  C  H  F  R  L  N  E  L  X
K  G  U  I  A  W  X  M  F  P  I  X  Y  D  S
P  P  Z  I  U  G  U  B  J  F  H  Y  R  N  E
H  H  C  J  V  J  B  H  C  Y  P  O  I  O  B
V  Z  N  M  W  F  A  P  T  X  U  E  T  X  V
```

Words Used

appealed

dealt

does

felt

girl

pealed

peeler

revealed

sealed

sealers

serial

steel

uphill

Day 100

Spelling Lesson:

As you hear them, write the spelling words for the day in the space provided. Be sure that you correct any words you have spelled incorrectly.

1._____

2._____

3._____

4._____

5._____

6._____

7._____

8._____

9._____

10._____

11._____

12._____

13._____

14._____

15._____

16._____

17._____

18._____

19._____

20._____

21._____

22._____

23._____

24._____

25._____

Using Your Words:

Choose at least five words from your spelling list and use them in a rhyme, silly story or sentences.

_____

_____

_____

_____

_____

_____

_____

_____

_____

_____

Day 101

Spelling Lesson:

As you hear them, write the spelling words for the day in the space provided. Be sure that you correct any words you have spelled incorrectly.

1._____

2._____

3._____

4._____

5._____

6._____

7._____

8._____

9._____

10. _____

11. _____

12. _____

13. _____

14. _____

15. _____

16. _____

17. _____

18. _____

19._____

20. _____

21. _____

22. _____

23. _____

24. _____

25. _____

Using Your Words:

List as many words as you can which have the following letters (in order) in them.

ook

_____

_____

_____

_____

_____

_____

_____

_____

_____

_____

Day 102

Spelling Lesson:

As you hear them, write the spelling words for the day in the space provided. Be sure that you correct any words you have spelled incorrectly.

1._____

2._____

3._____

4._____

5._____

6._____

7._____

8._____

9._____

10. _____

11. _____

12. _____

13. _____

14. _____

15. _____

16. _____

17. _____

18. _____

19._____

20. _____

21. _____

22. _____

23. _____

24. _____

25. _____

Using Your Words:

Fill in the blanks with words from today's spelling list.

1. When Julie c_____, she uses c_____.

2. How many r_____ are in a chess set?

3. C_____ sometimes c_____ the

b_____.

4. Alan and Jim gave the referees dirty l_____.

5. Doctors listen to patients describe their a_____ and pains.

6. Roadway Express Trucking has lots of 1.8. w_____ in their fleet.

7. How many b_____ baked those c_____?

8. Camouflage c_____ many servicemen.

Day 103

As you hear them, write the spelling words for the day in the space provided. Be sure that you correct any words you have spelled incorrectly.

1. _____

2. _____

3. _____

4. _____

5. _____

6. _____

7. _____

8. _____

9. _____

10. _____

11. _____

12. _____

13. _____

14. _____

15. _____

16. _____

17. _____

18. _____

19. _____

20. _____

21. _____

22. _____

23. _____

24. _____

25. _____

Using Your Words

Unscramble these:

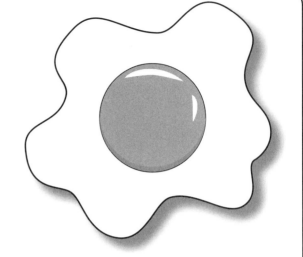

1. koobocok _____

2. krobo _____

3. aket _____

4. natek _____

5. noecaedlc _____

6. bareky _____

7. ovroeldoek_____

8. eigfeln _____

9. dheac _____

Day 104

Spelling Lesson:

As you hear them, write the spelling words for the day in the space provided. Be sure that you correct any words you have spelled incorrectly.

1. _____

2. _____

3. _____

4. _____

5. _____

6. _____

7. _____

8. _____

9. _____

10. _____

11. _____

12. _____

13. _____

14. _____

15. _____

16. _____

17. _____

18. _____

19. _____

20. _____

21. _____

22. _____

23. _____

24. _____

25. _____

Using Your Words:

Choose at least five words from your spelling list and use them in a rhyme, silly story or sentences.

_____

_____

_____

_____

_____

_____

_____

_____

_____

_____

Day 105

Spelling Lesson:

As you hear them, write the spelling words for the day in the space provided. Be sure that you correct any words you have spelled incorrectly.

1._____

2._____

3._____

4._____

5._____

6._____

7._____

8._____

9._____

10. _____

11. _____

12. _____

13. _____

14. _____

15. _____

16. _____

17. _____

18. _____

19._____

20. _____

21. _____

22. _____

23. _____

24. _____

25. _____

Using Your Words:

Sound-alike words

brake\break
stake\steak

Find the definitions of each of these sets of words and then use them in a sentence.

1._____

_____

2._____

_____

3._____

_____

4._____

_____

Sequential Spelling Level 1 - Student Workbook

Day 106

As you hear them, write the spelling words for the day in the space provided. Be sure that you correct any words you have spelled incorrectly.

1._____

2._____

3._____

4._____

5._____

6._____

7._____

8._____

9._____

10. _____

11. _____

12. _____

13. _____

14. _____

15. _____

16. _____

17. _____

18. _____

19._____

20. _____

21. _____

22. _____

23. _____

24. _____

25. _____

Using Your Words:

List as many words as you can that have the following letters (in order) in them.

ake

ache

_____

_____

_____

_____

_____

_____

_____

_____

_____

Day 107

Spelling Lesson:

As you hear them, write the spelling words for the day in the space provided. Be sure that you correct any words you have spelled incorrectly.

1. _____

2. _____

3. _____

4. _____

5. _____

6. _____

7. _____

8. _____

9. _____

10. _____

11. _____

12. _____

13. _____

14. _____

15. _____

16. _____

17. _____

18. _____

19. _____

20. _____

21. _____

22. _____

23. _____

24. _____

25. _____

Using Your Words:

Fill in the blanks with words from today's spelling list.

1. That _____ what I meant.

2. Who _____ these baked potatoes? They're great with my

_____!

3. Joan of Arc was burned at the _____.

4. After moving the piano, Jack and John _____ all over.

5. William Penn was a _____.

6. Rachel and Allison _____ the movie.

7. I called and called. My dog still _____ come.

8. Who _____ the window?

Day 108

Spelling Lesson:

As you hear them, write the spelling words for the day in the space provided. Be sure that you correct any words you have spelled incorrectly.

1. _____

2. _____

3. _____

4. _____

5. _____

6. _____

7. _____

8. _____

9. _____

10. _____

11. _____

12. _____

13. _____

14. _____

15. _____

16. _____

17. _____

18. _____

19. _____

20. _____

21. _____

22. _____

23. _____

24. _____

25. _____

Using Your Words

Can you find the words?

```
I  A  B  B  E  G  Q  Y  L  T  S  F  M  G  S
V  L  S  R  N  L  T  N  S  T  T  Z  F  N  E
Z  T  A  I  E  J  B  A  E  K  A  R  B  I  H
X  A  K  K  A  A  F  A  C  K  K  N  C  H  C
D  I  K  E  S  K  K  P  K  Q  E  Q  H  C  A
L  R  V  G  A  J  G  I  E  A  H  X  Y  A  H
U  I  O  E  A  R  Q  N  N  D  E  G  B  M  T
K  C  R  A  M  U  Z  X  I  G  A  R  D  T  O
T  B  A  N  A  Q  I  B  K  K  D  M  B  H  O
B  A  C  K  A  C  H  E  S  I  A  W  H  N  T
S  N  I  Z  A  I  V  N  Z  H  C  M  C  R  U
D  N  K  F  Z  L  H  X  E  Z  H  B  S  U  K
G  E  K  I  L  S  I  D  E  K  E  T  M  B  P
W  H  P  K  J  I  H  K  F  R  M  N  P  N  E
D  U  W  R  K  A  N  V  E  V  K  V  X  S  T
```

Words Used

aching

alike

backaches

brake

breakfast

breaking

dikes

dislike

headache

liking

made

making

quaking

stake

steak

toothaches

unbreakable

Day 109

As you hear them, write the spelling words for the day in the space provided. Be sure that you correct any words you have spelled incorrectly.

1._____

2._____

3._____

4._____

5._____

6._____

7._____

8._____

9._____

10. _____

11. _____

12. _____

13. _____

14. _____

15. _____

16. _____

17. _____

18. _____

19._____

20. _____

21. _____

22. _____

23. _____

24. _____

25. _____

Using Your Words:

Fill in the blanks with words from today's spelling list.

1. We went on a h_____ with M_____ and Jack.

2. Susan and Alaina laughed at Jim's j_____.

3. Wow! That's a lot of sm_____ from that forest fire.

4. Look at this egg. It has a double y_____.

5. A y_____ is used to harness oxen.

6. Who made that r_____?

7. Is that the new train s_____?

Sequential Spelling Level 1 - Student Workbook

Day 110

Spelling Lesson:

As you hear them, write the spelling words for the day in the space provided. Be sure that you correct any words you have spelled incorrectly.

1. _____

2. _____

3. _____

4. _____

5. _____

6. _____

7. _____

8. _____

9. _____

10. _____

11. _____

12. _____

13. _____

14. _____

15. _____

16. _____

17. _____

18. _____

19. _____

20. _____

21. _____

22. _____

23. _____

24. _____

25. _____

Using Your Words:

List as many words as you can with the following letters (in order) in them.

oke

ike

_____

_____

_____

_____

_____

_____

_____

_____

_____

Day 111

Spelling Lesson:

As you hear them, write the spelling words for the day in the space provided. Be sure that you correct any words you have spelled incorrectly.

1. _____

2. _____

3. _____

4. _____

5. _____

6. _____

7. _____

8. _____

9. _____

10. _____

11. _____

12. _____

13. _____

14. _____

15. _____

16. _____

17. _____

18. _____

19. _____

20. _____

21. _____

22. _____

23. _____

24. _____

25. _____

Using Your Words:

Unscramble these:

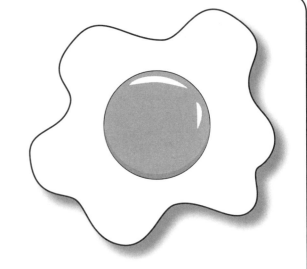

1. wodlu _____

2. dusloh _____

3. doluc _____

4. lowo _____

5. wllooy _____

6. vurroleed _____

7. suddeclhe _____

8. ketno _____

9. esokpn _____

Sequential Spelling Level 1 - Student Workbook

Day 112

Spelling Lesson:

As you hear them, write the spelling words for the day in the space provided. Be sure that you correct any words you have spelled incorrectly.

1._____

2._____

3._____

4._____

5._____

6._____

7._____

8._____

9._____

10. _____

11. _____

12. _____

13. _____

14. _____

15. _____

16. _____

17. _____

18. _____

19._____

20. _____

21. _____

22. _____

23. _____

24. _____

25. _____

Using Your Words:

Choose at least five words from your spelling list and use each in a sentence.

1._____

_____

2._____

_____

3._____

_____

4._____

_____

5._____

_____

Day 113

Spelling Lesson:

As you hear them, write the spelling words for the day in the space provided. Be sure that you correct any words you have spelled incorrectly.

1.＿＿＿＿＿＿＿＿＿＿＿

2.＿＿＿＿＿＿＿＿＿＿＿

3.＿＿＿＿＿＿＿＿＿＿＿

4.＿＿＿＿＿＿＿＿＿＿＿

5.＿＿＿＿＿＿＿＿＿＿＿

6.＿＿＿＿＿＿＿＿＿＿＿

7.＿＿＿＿＿＿＿＿＿＿＿

8.＿＿＿＿＿＿＿＿＿＿＿

9.＿＿＿＿＿＿＿＿＿＿＿

10. ＿＿＿＿＿＿＿＿＿＿

11. ＿＿＿＿＿＿＿＿＿＿

12. ＿＿＿＿＿＿＿＿＿＿

13. ＿＿＿＿＿＿＿＿＿＿

14. ＿＿＿＿＿＿＿＿＿＿

15. ＿＿＿＿＿＿＿＿＿＿

16. ＿＿＿＿＿＿＿＿＿＿

17. ＿＿＿＿＿＿＿＿＿＿

18. ＿＿＿＿＿＿＿＿＿＿

19. ＿＿＿＿＿＿＿＿＿＿

20. ＿＿＿＿＿＿＿＿＿＿

21. ＿＿＿＿＿＿＿＿＿＿

22. ＿＿＿＿＿＿＿＿＿＿

23. ＿＿＿＿＿＿＿＿＿＿

24. ＿＿＿＿＿＿＿＿＿＿

25. ＿＿＿＿＿＿＿＿＿＿

Using Your Words:

Sound-alike words

dear\deer
hear\here
peer\pier

Find the definitions of each of these sets of words and then use them in a sentence.

1._____

_____

2._____

_____

3._____

_____

4._____

_____

5._____

_____

6._____

_____

Day 114

Spelling Lesson:

As you hear them, write the spelling words for the day in the space provided. Be sure that you correct any words you have spelled incorrectly.

1._____

2._____

3._____

4._____

5._____

6._____

7._____

8._____

9._____

10. _____

11. _____

12. _____

13. _____

14. _____

15. _____

16. _____

17. _____

18. _____

19._____

20. _____

21. _____

22. _____

23. _____

24. _____

25. _____

Using Your Words:

List as many words as you can that have the following letters (in order) in them.

ear

eer

_____

_____

_____

_____

_____

_____

_____

_____

_____

Spelling Lesson:

As you hear them, write the spelling words for the day in the space provided. Be sure that you correct any words you have spelled incorrectly.

1._____

2._____

3._____

4._____

5._____

6._____

7._____

8._____

9._____

10. _____

11. _____

12. _____

13. _____

14. _____

15. _____

16. _____

17. _____

18. _____

19._____

20. _____

21. _____

22. _____

23. _____

24. _____

25. _____

Using Your Words:

Fill in the blanks with words from today's spelling list.

1. I _____ you the first time you called.

2. Alison lost an _____.

3. Tim _____ Jack and Liz talking about his surprise party.

4. _____ you finished your homework yet?

5. My mom _____ the floor with me when I was fussy.

6. Yesterday, we discovered that someone had _____ the statue with graffiti.

7. Every kindergartner should know how to tie a _____.

8. Let's go _____ quiet.

Day 116

As you hear them, write the spelling words for the day in the space provided. Be sure that you correct any words you have spelled incorrectly.

1._____

2._____

3._____

4._____

5._____

6._____

7._____

8._____

9._____

10. _____

11. _____

12. _____

13. _____

14. _____

15. _____

16. _____

17. _____

18. _____

19._____

20. _____

21. _____

22. _____

23. _____

24. _____

25. _____

Using Your Words

Can you find the words?

```
U F Z F O W K F D F D K Q Z K
N D Z H E W Q E A E B I Q Y I
L S T A C W L U R M J J Z E V
Q O R Q X B L A O U X P G J L
Q Y U W K H E A R D Z L H G H
Z U P T X G F T Z D Z M Z U E
J B E T A F U E I U W N B I Q
U M R E S I B E M P P E G S Y
D O V E R H E A R D A A I Z Z
X E R E H R O Z U R C R H N E
D E R E E H C E D N E R H S C
E I R E E T H E L S D I J A A
B E F F E D D N S A E N Z Y F
P Y B V X N M N L G C G Z M E
G W G S X J S O H R A E L J D
```

Words Used

aced

bearded

cheered

deer

deface

earring

eerie

geared

heard

overheard

paced

queer

shoelace

sneered

weary

Day 117

Spelling Lesson:

As you hear them, write the spelling words for the day in the space provided. Be sure that you correct any words you have spelled incorrectly.

1._____

2._____

3._____

4._____

5._____

6._____

7._____

8._____

9._____

10. _____

11. _____

12. _____

13. _____

14. _____

15. _____

16. _____

17. _____

18. _____

19._____

20. _____

21. _____

22. _____

23. _____

24. _____

25. _____

Using Your Words:

List as many words as possible with the following letters (in order) in them.

ace

_____

_____

_____

_____

_____

_____

_____

_____

_____

_____

Day 118

Spelling Lesson:

As you hear them, write the spelling words for the day in the space provided. Be sure that you correct any words you have spelled incorrectly.

1._____

2._____

3._____

4._____

5._____

6._____

7._____

8._____

9._____

10._____

11._____

12._____

13._____

14._____

15._____

16._____

17._____

18._____

19._____

20._____

21._____

22._____

23._____

24._____

25._____

Using Your Words:

Sound-alike and look-alike words

tear\tier "TEER"
tear "TAY'r"
sheer\shear

Find the definitions of each of these words and then use them in a sentence.

1._____

_____

2._____

_____

3._____

_____

4._____

_____

Day 119

Spelling Lesson:

As you hear them, write the spelling words for the day in the space provided. Be sure that you correct any words you have spelled incorrectly.

1. _____

2. _____

3. _____

4. _____

5. _____

6. _____

7. _____

8. _____

9. _____

10. _____

11. _____

12. _____

13. _____

14. _____

15. _____

16. _____

17. _____

18. _____

19. _____

20. _____

21. _____

22. _____

23. _____

24. _____

25. _____

Using Your Words

Fill in the blanks with words from today's spelling list.

1. The tornado _____ off part of our roof.

2. He _____ without saying good-bye.

3. What _____ this remind you of?

4. As we rounded the turn, there was a _____ cliff.

5. Many people were _____ as a result of the civil war in Bosnia.

6. Rose _____ to go first.

7. Dr. Michael DeBakey was one of the surgeons who _____ the artificial heart.

8. Are you thinking about teaching as a _____?

Day 120

As you hear them, write the spelling words for the day in the space provided. Be sure that you correct any words you have spelled incorrectly.

1._____

2._____

3._____

4._____

5._____

6._____

7._____

8._____

9._____

10._____

11._____

12._____

13._____

14._____

15._____

16._____

17._____

18._____

19._____

20._____

21._____

22._____

23._____

24._____

25._____

Using Your Words

Choose at least five words from your spelling list and use each in a sentence.

1._____

_____

2._____

_____

3._____

_____

4._____

_____

5._____

_____

Evaluation Test #3

1. Those kids are always f_____.

2. That means they're always misbeh_____.

3. It's time for them to turn over a new l_____.

4. I thought it was time to rake the l_____.

5. It's time we sh_____ into high gear.

6. We're going to be inst_____ a new system.

7. My sister likes to f_____ up our gas tank.

8. I liked math about h_____ the time.

9. We keep our medicine on the highest sh_____.

10. It was the b_____ jug I've ever seen.

11. They dr_____ a new well last week.

12. How are you f_____ today?

13. Too many c_____ spoil the broth.

14. They are always squ_____ their tires.

15. They were sh_____ in their boots.

16. We h_____ all the way into town.

17. Sm_____ is not allowed in most public places.

18. Everybody has r_____ that they are to follow.

19. My brother is very hard of h_____.

20. Do we have any volunt_____?

Day 121

As you hear them, write the spelling words for the day in the space provided. Be sure that you correct any words you have spelled incorrectly.

1. _____

2. _____

3. _____

4. _____

5. _____

6. _____

7. _____

8. _____

9. _____

10. _____

11. _____

12. _____

13. _____

14. _____

15. _____

16. _____

17. _____

18. _____

19. _____

20. _____

21. _____

22. _____

23. _____

24. _____

25. _____

Using Your Words:

List as many words as you can with the following letters (in order) in them.

ice

ang

_____

_____

_____

_____

_____

_____

_____

_____

_____

Day 122

As you hear them, write the spelling words for the day in the space provided. Be sure that you correct any words you have spelled incorrectly.

1. _____

2. _____

3. _____

4. _____

5. _____

6. _____

7. _____

8. _____

9. _____

10. _____

11. _____

12. _____

13. _____

14. _____

15. _____

16. _____

17. _____

18. _____

19. _____

20. _____

21. _____

22. _____

23. _____

24. _____

25. _____

Using Your Words:

Unscramble these:

1. rsrtcaee _____

2. dcie _____

3. asecp _____

4. irscep _____

5. eiwtc _____

6. gsgan _____

7. galcn _____

8. nhgsare _____

9. dposl _____

Day 123

Spelling Lesson:

As you hear them, write the spelling words for the day in the space provided. Be sure that you correct any words you have spelled incorrectly.

1._____

2._____

3._____

4._____

5._____

6._____

7._____

8._____

9._____

10. _____

11. _____

12. _____

13. _____

14. _____

15. _____

16. _____

17. _____

18. _____

19._____

20. _____

21. _____

22. _____

23. _____

24. _____

25. _____

Using Your Words

Fill in the blanks with words from today's spelling list.

1. We _____ our steps to see if we could find her glasses.

2. Julie _____ the cupcakes.

3. I found _____ in the attic.

4. The bell _____ furiously.

5. H_____ you heard that a_____ before?

6. At 11:30, I felt a hunger _____.

7. Aunt Betty s_____ her pumpkin pie.

8. I'm not sure that this desk is _____ to sell.

9. Last Saturday, I _____ off during the movie.

10. Our horses _____ slowly towards the barn.

Day 124

Spelling Lesson:

As you hear them, write the spelling words for the day in the space provided. Be sure that you correct any words you have spelled incorrectly.

1._____

2._____

3._____

4._____

5._____

6._____

7._____

8._____

9._____

10. _____

11. _____

12. _____

13. _____

14. _____

15. _____

16. _____

17. _____

18. _____

19._____

20. _____

21. _____

22. _____

23. _____

24. _____

25. _____

Using Your Words:

Choose at least five words from your spelling list and write a silly story or poem using them.

Day 125

As you hear them, write the spelling words for the day in the space provided. Be sure that you correct any words you have spelled incorrectly.

1._____

2._____

3._____

4._____

5._____

6._____

7._____

8._____

9._____

10. _____

11. _____

12. _____

13. _____

14. _____

15. _____

16. _____

17. _____

18. _____

19._____

20. _____

21. _____

22. _____

23. _____

24. _____

25. _____

Using Your Words:

Fill in the blanks with words from today's spelling list.

1. I'm as snug as a b_____ in a r_____ under my quilt.

2. The s_____ came into town dressed in black.

3. Alicia went to _____ her clothes so we could go swimming.

4. Please p_____ the tray on the table.

5. I_____ goes into a computer; o_____ comes out.

6. My dad is helping build the new tollway _____.

7. Sheila and Nancy need to s_____ in the flower _____

for her surprise.

Day 126

Spelling Lesson:

As you hear them, write the spelling words for the day in the space provided. Be sure that you correct any words you have spelled incorrectly.

1._____

2._____

3._____

4._____

5._____

6._____

7._____

8._____

9._____

10. _____

11. _____

12. _____

13. _____

14. _____

15. _____

16. _____

17. _____

18. _____

19._____

20. _____

21. _____

22. _____

23. _____

24. _____

25. _____

Using Your Words

List as many words as you can think of that have the following letters (in order) in them.

ug

ange

Day 127

As you hear them, write the spelling words for the day in the space provided. Be sure that you correct any words you have spelled incorrectly.

1._____

2._____

3._____

4._____

5._____

6._____

7._____

8._____

9._____

10. _____

11. _____

12. _____

13. _____

14. _____

15. _____

16. _____

17. _____

18. _____

19._____

20. _____

21. _____

22. _____

23. _____

24. _____

25. _____

Using Your Words:

Unscramble these:

1. gbdgue   _____

2. gregud   _____

3. nstsrateg   _____

4. gsgmingul   _____

5. nedaearrrg   _____

6. xdngaheec   _____

7. dcenartngihe   _____

8. utp   _____

Day 128

Spelling Lesson:

As you hear them, write the spelling words for the day in the space provided. Be sure that you correct any words you have spelled incorrectly.

1._____

2._____

3._____

4._____

5._____

6._____

7._____

8._____

9._____

10. _____

11. _____

12. _____

13. _____

14. _____

15. _____

16. _____

17. _____

18. _____

19._____

20. _____

21. _____

22. _____

23. _____

24. _____

25. _____

Using Your Words:

Tricky words

putting "PuuT ing"
putting "P'ut ting"

Use each of these words correctly in a sentence.

1._____

_____

2._____

_____

Day 129

Spelling Lesson:

As you hear them, write the spelling words for the day in the space provided. Be sure that you correct any words you have spelled incorrectly.

1._____

2._____

3._____

4._____

5._____

6._____

7._____

8._____

9._____

10. _____

11. _____

12. _____

13. _____

14. _____

15. _____

16. _____

17. _____

18. _____

19._____

20. _____

21. _____

22. _____

23. _____

24. _____

25. _____

Using Your Words:

Sound-alike words   **but\butt**   Use each of these words correctly in a sentence.

1._____

_____

2._____

_____

Day 130

Spelling Lesson:

As you hear them, write the spelling words for the day in the space provided. Be sure that you correct any words you have spelled incorrectly.

1._____

2._____

3._____

4._____

5._____

6._____

7._____

8._____

9._____

10._____

11._____

12._____

13._____

14._____

15._____

16._____

17._____

18._____

19._____

20._____

21._____

22._____

23._____

24._____

25._____

Using Your Words:

Unscramble these:

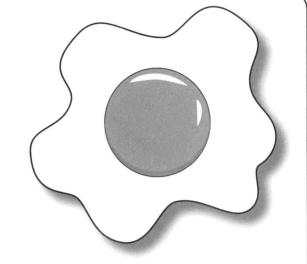

1. mugegr _____

2. sgulserg _____

3. tbtu _____

4. uhst _____

5. tshletu _____

6. ontbtu _____

7. dsik _____

8. odrifb _____

9. dlyptius _____

Day 131

Spelling Lesson:

As you hear them, write the spelling words for the day in the space provided. Be sure that you correct any words you have spelled incorrectly.

1._____

2._____

3._____

4._____

5._____

6._____

7._____

8._____

9._____

10. _____

11. _____

12. _____

13. _____

14. _____

15. _____

16. _____

17. _____

18. _____

19._____

20. _____

21. _____

22. _____

23. _____

24. _____

25. _____

Using Your Words:

Fill in the blanks with words from today's spelling list.

1. Did you hear that John got m_____ last night?

2. The fire g_____ their house.

3. Alex k_____ me about my new glasses.

4. I really p_____ well on the golf course today.

5. Sugar is f_____ for diabetics.

6. Hello! _____ you come in?

7. D_____ she look nice?

8. The car s_____ to a stop on the ice.

Day 132

Spelling Lesson:

As you hear them, write the spelling words for the day in the space provided. Be sure that you correct any words you have spelled incorrectly.

1._____

2._____

3._____

4._____

5._____

6._____

7._____

8._____

9._____

10. _____

11. _____

12. _____

13. _____

14. _____

15. _____

16. _____

17. _____

18. _____

19. _____

20. _____

21. _____

22. _____

23. _____

24. _____

25. _____

Using Your Words

Can you **find** the words?

```
S  C  N  M  Y  D  P  Z  N  U  Q  P  T  B  C
O  L  E  E  E  X  V  L  J  L  C  Z  V  C  F
Y  H  U  G  Y  M  Y  I  C  O  N  O  U  L  F
R  C  G  G  T  T  U  S  F  N  D  B  M  F  W
N  U  B  U  G  K  E  Q  U  D  O  M  O  Q  K
T  L  S  J  Y  I  W  J  E  R  M  M  C  N  B
D  W  P  O  N  G  S  N  S  N  U  G  L  Y  E
D  E  O  U  Z  O  O  H  B  I  G  Z  W  N  M
W  L  D  R  T  T  C  U  O  H  G  Q  S  U  H
O  L  W  D  T  T  T  D  G  N  I  T  T  U  P
O  V  V  U  I  T  Y  I  M  T  N  T  N  B  B
G  L  B  H  I  K  P  P  I  O  G  F  S  F  O
Z  N  C  N  M  S  H  U  T  T  L  I  N  G  I
U  F  G  X  R  U  R  T  X  O  W  P  U  D  E
M  V  O  Y  H  E  E  S  E  M  B  N  G  R  U
```

Words Used

butting

kidded

mugging

mutt

putting

putty

shuttling

sluggish

snug

snugly

stupid

tugged

unbuttoned

Day 133

As you hear them, write the spelling words for the day in the space provided. Be sure that you correct any words you have spelled incorrectly.

1._____

2._____

3._____

4._____

5._____

6._____

7._____

8._____

9._____

10. _____

11. _____

12. _____

13. _____

14. _____

15. _____

16. _____

17. _____

18. _____

19._____

20. _____

21. _____

22. _____

23. _____

24. _____

25. _____

Using Your Words:

List as many words as you can with the following letters (in order) in them.

ide

id

Spelling Lesson:

As you hear them, write the spelling words for the day in the space provided. Be sure that you correct any words you have spelled incorrectly.

1._____

2._____

3._____

4._____

5._____

6._____

7._____

8._____

9._____

10. _____

11. _____

12. _____

13. _____

14. _____

15. _____

16. _____

17. _____

18. _____

19._____

20. _____

21. _____

22. _____

23. _____

24. _____

25. _____

Using Your Words:

Sound-alike words

pride\pried
its\it's; two\to\too

Use each of these words correctly in a sentence.

_____

_____

_____

_____

_____

_____

_____

_____

_____

_____

Day 135

Spelling Lesson:

As you hear them, write the spelling words for the day in the space provided. Be sure that you correct any words you have spelled incorrectly.

1._____

2._____

3._____

4._____

5._____

6._____

7._____

8._____

9._____

10. _____

11. _____

12. _____

13. _____

14. _____

15. _____

16. _____

17. _____

18. _____

19._____

20. _____

21. _____

22. _____

23. _____

24. _____

25. _____

Using Your Words:

Fill in the blanks with words from today's spelling list.

1. I r_____ in the ambulance.

2. Julie p_____ herself on her clean room.

3. When Michael Jordan s_____ onto the basketball court, heads turned.

4. That was a s_____ mistake.

5. Dan f_____ with the tuner on the radio.

6. Q_____ is the British term for a British pound.

7. The cows m_____ when it was time for milking.

8. That's a s_____ idea!

Day 136

Spelling Lesson:

As you hear them, write the spelling words for the day in the space provided. Be sure that you correct any words you have spelled incorrectly.

1._____

2._____

3._____

4._____

5._____

6._____

7._____

8._____

9._____

10. _____

11. _____

12. _____

13. _____

14. _____

15. _____

16. _____

17. _____

18. _____

19._____

20. _____

21. _____

22. _____

23. _____

24. _____

25. _____

Using Your Words:

Choose at least seven words from your spelling list and use each in a sentence.

1._____

_____

2._____

_____

3._____

_____

4._____

_____

5._____

_____

6._____

_____

7._____

_____

Day 137

As you hear them, write the spelling words for the day in the space provided. Be sure that you correct any words you have spelled incorrectly.

1._____

2._____

3._____

4._____

5._____

6._____

7._____

8._____

9._____

10. _____

11. _____

12. _____

13. _____

14. _____

15. _____

16. _____

17. _____

18. _____

19._____

20. _____

21. _____

22. _____

23. _____

24. _____

25. _____

Using Your Words:

Sound-alike words

shoe\shoo
side\sighed

Use each of these words correctly in a sentence.

1._____

_____

2._____

_____

3._____

_____

4._____

_____

Day 138

Spelling Lesson:

As you hear them, write the spelling words for the day in the space provided. Be sure that you correct any words you have spelled incorrectly.

1._____

2._____

3._____

4._____

5._____

6._____

7._____

8._____

9._____

10. _____

11. _____

12. _____

13. _____

14. _____

15. _____

16. _____

17. _____

18. _____

19._____

20. _____

21. _____

22. _____

23. _____

24. _____

25. _____

Using Your Words:

Find the meaning of the following words and use each in a sentence.

1.decisive _____

_____

2.taboos _____

_____

3.provides_____

_____

4.collides_____

_____

5. gooey _____

_____

Day 139

As you hear them, write the spelling words for the day in the space provided. Be sure that you correct any words you have spelled incorrectly.

1._____

2._____

3._____

4._____

5._____

6._____

7._____

8._____

9._____

10. _____

11. _____

12. _____

13. _____

14. _____

15. _____

16. _____

17. _____

18. _____

19._____

20. _____

21. _____

22. _____

23. _____

24. _____

25. _____

Using Your Words:

Unscramble these:

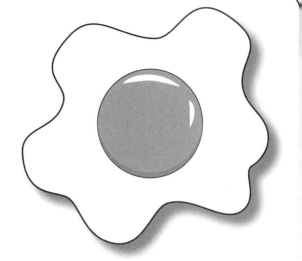

1. weiyads   _____

2. cdideydel   _____

3. psoodahme _____

4. olgio   _____

5. dlwuo   _____

6. soobhex   _____

7. oneac   _____

8. ardeewt   _____

9. iseind   _____

10. vrpingiod   _____

Day 140

As you hear them, write the spelling words for the day in the space provided. Be sure that you correct any words you have spelled incorrectly.

1._____

2._____

3._____

4._____

5._____

6._____

7._____

8._____

9._____

10. _____

11. _____

12. _____

13. _____

14. _____

15. _____

16. _____

17. _____

18. _____

19._____

20. _____

21. _____

22. _____

23. _____

24. _____

25. _____

Using Your Words:

Choose at least seven words from your spelling list and use them in a short paragraph, silly story or poem.

_____

_____

_____

_____

_____

_____

_____

_____

_____

_____

Sequential Spelling Level I - Student Workbook

Day 141

As you hear them, write the spelling words for the day in the space provided. Be sure that you correct any words you have spelled incorrectly.

1._____

2._____

3._____

4._____

5._____

6._____

7._____

8._____

9._____

10. _____

11. _____

12. _____

13. _____

14. _____

15. _____

16. _____

17. _____

18. _____

19._____

20. _____

21. _____

22. _____

23. _____

24. _____

25. _____

Using Your Words:

Fill in the blanks with words from today's spelling list.

1. The temperature outside is z_____degrees. It's cold!

2. The t_____is coming in.

3. Who is your _____?

4. That is a lovely p_____ s_____ you're playing.

5. Cowboys use a l_____ to catch b_____.

6. In the summer, we have parties on our p_____.

7. I'm _____ you will do well on the test.

8. Is she a r_____here?

Day 142

Spelling Lesson:

As you hear them, write the spelling words for the day in the space provided. Be sure that you correct any words you have spelled incorrectly.

1. _____

2. _____

3. _____

4. _____

5. _____

6. _____

7. _____

8. _____

9. _____

10. _____

11. _____

12. _____

13. _____

14. _____

15. _____

16. _____

17. _____

18. _____

19. _____

20. _____

21. _____

22. _____

23. _____

24. _____

25. _____

Using Your Words:

Sound-alike words

residents\residence
no\know
tide\tied

Use each of these words correctly in a sentence.

1._____

_____

2._____

_____

3._____

_____

4._____

_____

5._____

_____

6._____

_____

Day 143

Spelling Lesson:

As you hear them, write the spelling words for the day in the space provided. Be sure that you correct any words you have spelled incorrectly.

1._____

2._____

3._____

4._____

5._____

6._____

7._____

8._____

9._____

10. _____

11. _____

12. _____

13. _____

14. _____

15. _____

16. _____

17. _____

18. _____

19._____

20. _____

21. _____

22. _____

23. _____

24. _____

25. _____

Using Your Words:

go, gone, went

Go is the present tense (the action of "going" is happening now)
Went is the past tense (the action has already happened)
Gone is the past tense which is used after the following words
(have, had, has, is, or any form of be).

Fill in the blanks using go, goes, going, went or gone.

1. The baby _____ to sleep an hour ago.

2. They are _____ to the airport soon.

3. Where have my keys _____?

4. Alan _____ to school on the bus.

5. Let's _____ fishing tomorrow.

6. We used to _____ sailing on weekends.

7. Allison _____ to the party by herself.

8. We have already _____ to the store.

9. Do you want to _____ shopping with me?

Day 144

Spelling Lesson:

As you hear them, write the spelling words for the day in the space provided. Be sure that you correct any words you have spelled incorrectly.

1._____

2._____

3._____

4._____

5._____

6._____

7._____

8._____

9._____

10. _____

11. _____

12. _____

13. _____

14. _____

15. _____

16. _____

17. _____

18. _____

19._____

20. _____

21. _____

22. _____

23. _____

24. _____

25. _____

Using Your Words:

Can you find the words?

```
S  M  G  S  N  J  Z  G  X  S  E  Y  U  C  G
E  T  X  G  R  X  O  B  E  N  W  M  O  Y  U
O  B  N  X  U  I  Z  O  M  J  M  N  D  Q  I
T  E  J  E  N  I  T  C  E  L  F  D  R  S  D
A  L  C  G  D  A  V  E  Z  I  P  T  K  K  E
M  E  O  H  T  I  R  X  D  B  W  C  W  T  D
O  M  H  O  O  H  S  E  S  O  L  O  I  N  G
T  S  P  O  V  E  N  E  B  P  A  P  P  C  S
L  E  L  R  D  T  D  T  R  S  O  R  E  Z  Z
L  N  L  A  I  T  N  E  D  I  S  E  R  P  I
L  O  M  A  F  E  S  L  G  S  B  T  I  D  E
G  G  L  S  W  A  B  L  N  P  O  O  S  P  D
M  L  G  L  K  E  Q  Y  H  W  Y  D  M  C  A
Y  Y  L  K  U  Q  J  A  G  U  N  V  D  L  X
U  G  N  Z  H  X  G  T  A  Q  K  F  X  F  F
```

Words Used

also

confidentially

echoed

going

gone

guided

potatoes

presidential

residents

soloing

tide

tomatoes

went

zeros

Day 145

Spelling Lesson:

As you hear them, write the spelling words for the day in the space provided. Be sure that you correct any words you have spelled incorrectly.

1. _____

2. _____

3. _____

4. _____

5. _____

6. _____

7. _____

8. _____

9. _____

10. _____

11. _____

12. _____

13. _____

14. _____

15. _____

16. _____

17. _____

18. _____

19. _____

20. _____

21. _____

22. _____

23. _____

24. _____

25. _____

Using Your Words:

List as many words as possible with the following letters (in order) in them.

oe

ow ("OW")

Day 146

As you hear them, write the spelling words for the day in the space provided. Be sure that you correct any words you have spelled incorrectly.

1._____

2._____

3._____

4._____

5._____

6._____

7._____

8._____

9._____

10._____

11._____

12._____

13._____

14._____

15._____

16._____

17._____

18._____

19._____

20._____

21._____

22._____

23._____

24._____

25._____

Using Your Words:

Sound-alike words

> **doe/dough**
> **tow/toe**
> **know/no**

Look alike words

does "DOH'z" = the plural form of **doe,** a female deer

does "DUHZ" = a form of the verb **do**

Use each of these words correctly in a sentence.

1._____

_____

2._____

_____

3._____

_____

4._____

_____

5._____

_____

6._____

_____

7._____

_____

8._____

_____

Day 147

As you hear them, write the spelling words for the day in the space provided. Be sure that you correct any words you have spelled incorrectly.

1._____

2._____

3._____

4._____

5._____

6._____

7._____

8._____

9._____

10. _____

11. _____

12. _____

13. _____

14. _____

15. _____

16. _____

17. _____

18. _____

19._____

20. _____

21. _____

22. _____

23. _____

24. _____

25. _____

Using Your Words:

Fill in the blanks with words from today's spelling list.

1. _____ coming to dinner?

2. I _____ finish this project today.

3. My aunt was amazed at how big I've _____.

4. Jake _____ the whistle.

5. Our car had to be _____ to the repair shop because a tire had

_____.

6. Do you know _____ book this is?

7. The Mississippi _____ its banks this spring.

8. Grandpa has _____ in his old age.

Spelling Lesson:

As you hear them, write the spelling words for the day in the space provided. Be sure that you correct any words you have spelled incorrectly.

1._____

2._____

3._____

4._____

5._____

6._____

7._____

8._____

9._____

10. _____

11. _____

12. _____

13. _____

14. _____

15. _____

16. _____

17. _____

18. _____

19._____

20. _____

21. _____

22. _____

23. _____

24. _____

25. _____

Using Your Words:

Choose at least seven words from your spelling list and use them in a short paragraph, silly story or poem.

_____

_____

_____

_____

_____

_____

_____

_____

_____

_____

Day 149

As you hear them, write the spelling words for the day in the space provided. Be sure that you correct any words you have spelled incorrectly.

1._____

2._____

3._____

4._____

5._____

6._____

7._____

8._____

9._____

10. _____

11. _____

12. _____

13. _____

14. _____

15. _____

16. _____

17. _____

18. _____

19._____

20. _____

21. _____

22. _____

23. _____

24. _____

25. _____

Using Your Words:

Sound-alike words

bow\bough
plow\plough

Look alike words: **bow "B'OW" or "B'OH"**
sow "S'OW" or "S'OH" Use each of these words
correctly in a sentence.

1._____

_____

2._____

_____

3._____

_____

4._____

_____

5._____

_____

6._____

_____

7._____

_____

8._____

_____

Day 150

Spelling Lesson:

As you hear them, write the spelling words for the day in the space provided. Be sure that you correct any words you have spelled incorrectly.

1._____

2._____

3._____

4._____

5._____

6._____

7._____

8._____

9._____

10. _____

11. _____

12. _____

13. _____

14. _____

15. _____

16. _____

17. _____

18. _____

19._____

20. _____

21. _____

22. _____

23. _____

24. _____

25. _____

Using Your Words:

List as many words as possible with the following letters (in order) in them.

ow ("OH")

_____

_____

_____

_____

_____

_____

_____

_____

_____

Spelling Lesson:

As you hear them, write the spelling words for the day in the space provided. Be sure that you correct any words you have spelled incorrectly.

1._____

2._____

3._____

4._____

5._____

6._____

7._____

8._____

9._____

10. _____

11. _____

12. _____

13. _____

14. _____

15. _____

16. _____

17. _____

18. _____

19._____

20. _____

21. _____

22. _____

23. _____

24. _____

25. _____

Using Your Words:

Sound-alike words
Fill in the blanks.

so\sew\sow
threw\through
thrown\throne

1. _____, where did you go last night?

2. Who _____ that snowball _____ the window?

3. Guys should learn to _____ buttons as well as girls.

4. Queen Elizabeth has been on the _____ for over fifty years.

5. She was _____ from the horse.

6. When will you _____ the wheat field?

Day 152

Spelling Lesson:

As you hear them, write the spelling words for the day in the space provided. Be sure that you correct any words you have spelled incorrectly.

1._____

2._____

3._____

4._____

5._____

6._____

7._____

8._____

9._____

10. _____

11. _____

12. _____

13. _____

14. _____

15. _____

16. _____

17. _____

18. _____

19._____

20. _____

21. _____

22. _____

23. _____

24. _____

25. _____

Using Your Words:

Choose at least seven words from your spelling list and use them in a short paragraph, silly story or poem.

_____

_____

_____

_____

_____

_____

_____

_____

_____

_____

Day 153

Spelling Lesson:

As you hear them, write the spelling words for the day in the space provided. Be sure that you correct any words you have spelled incorrectly.

1._____

2._____

3._____

4._____

5._____

6._____

7._____

8._____

9._____

10. _____

11. _____

12. _____

13. _____

14. _____

15. _____

16. _____

17. _____

18. _____

19._____

20. _____

21. _____

22. _____

23. _____

24. _____

25. _____

Using Your Words:

Sound-alike words

please\pleas
medal\meddle
pedal\peddle

Use each of these words correctly in a sentence.

1._____

_____

2._____

_____

3._____

_____

4._____

_____

5._____

_____

6._____

_____

Day 154

As you hear them, write the spelling words for the day in the space provided. Be sure that you correct any words you have spelled incorrectly.

1._____

2._____

3._____

4._____

5._____

6._____

7._____

8._____

9._____

10. _____

11. _____

12. _____

13. _____

14. _____

15. _____

16. _____

17. _____

18. _____

19._____

20. _____

21. _____

22. _____

23. _____

24. _____

25. _____

Using Your Words:

List as many words as you can that have the following letters (in order) in them.

ad

ease

_____

_____

_____

_____

_____

_____

_____

_____

_____

Spelling Lesson:

As you hear them, write the spelling words for the day in the space provided. Be sure that you correct any words you have spelled incorrectly.

1._____

2._____

3._____

4._____

5._____

6._____

7._____

8._____

9._____

10. _____

11. _____

12. _____

13. _____

14. _____

15. _____

16. _____

17. _____

18. _____

19._____

20. _____

21. _____

22. _____

23. _____

24. _____

25. _____

Using Your Words:

Unscramble these:

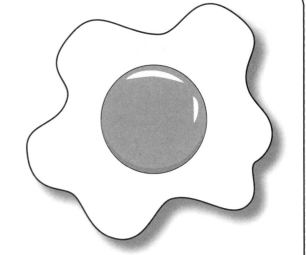

1. seastei   _____

2. seapled   _____

3. ssdiapdeel _____

4. leddra   _____

5. eptla   _____

6. dedldem _____

7. eisczdpa _____

8. wdeedd   _____

9. daseiesd _____

10. lgaednss _____

Day 156

As you hear them, write the spelling words for the day in the space provided. Be sure that you correct any words you have spelled incorrectly.

1._____

2._____

3._____

4._____

5._____

6._____

7._____

8._____

9._____

10._____

11._____

12._____

13._____

14._____

15._____

16._____

17._____

18._____

19._____

20._____

21._____

22._____

23._____

24._____

25._____

Using Your Words:

Can you find the words?

```
B T L F U L P S E Z E G Y Z A
I Q S W A L C L H L T N S A K
T D A E E M H Z D E P I A I A
A G L X I R M D G L M D E J I
C U B R E S E Q E I P D P C M
E B D U C P A A R M A E J E E
I S N W P Y S E N W A W E C T
Z T A E V U K S C S H D G X A
F H D E R E S A E S I D L I L
U A C E B T J G L I W G Z Y H
L M I D E L B I V I O M A D K
M T Y P L E A S E D H I E C P
A G Q A C N Q S A C H C H R V
Y Q N C E C V L K Q Y B Q L D
Q N I H E E G S I Z E Q S Y Z
```

Words Used

bled

disease

ease

easiest

easy

glad

madly

metal

pedal

peddle

please

pleasure

she

size

wedding

Spelling Lesson:

As you hear them, write the spelling words for the day in the space provided. Be sure that you correct any words you have spelled incorrectly.

1.＿＿＿＿＿＿＿＿＿＿＿＿＿＿

2.＿＿＿＿＿＿＿＿＿＿＿＿＿＿

3.＿＿＿＿＿＿＿＿＿＿＿＿＿＿

4.＿＿＿＿＿＿＿＿＿＿＿＿＿＿

5.＿＿＿＿＿＿＿＿＿＿＿＿＿＿

6.＿＿＿＿＿＿＿＿＿＿＿＿＿＿

7.＿＿＿＿＿＿＿＿＿＿＿＿＿＿

8.＿＿＿＿＿＿＿＿＿＿＿＿＿＿

9.＿＿＿＿＿＿＿＿＿＿＿＿＿＿

10. ＿＿＿＿＿＿＿＿＿＿＿＿＿

11. ＿＿＿＿＿＿＿＿＿＿＿＿＿

12. ＿＿＿＿＿＿＿＿＿＿＿＿＿

13. ＿＿＿＿＿＿＿＿＿＿＿＿＿

14. ＿＿＿＿＿＿＿＿＿＿＿＿＿

15. ＿＿＿＿＿＿＿＿＿＿＿＿＿

16. ＿＿＿＿＿＿＿＿＿＿＿＿＿

17. ＿＿＿＿＿＿＿＿＿＿＿＿＿

18. ＿＿＿＿＿＿＿＿＿＿＿＿＿

19.＿＿＿＿＿＿＿＿＿＿＿＿＿

20. ＿＿＿＿＿＿＿＿＿＿＿＿＿

21. ＿＿＿＿＿＿＿＿＿＿＿＿＿

22. ＿＿＿＿＿＿＿＿＿＿＿＿＿

23. ＿＿＿＿＿＿＿＿＿＿＿＿＿

24. ＿＿＿＿＿＿＿＿＿＿＿＿＿

25. ＿＿＿＿＿＿＿＿＿＿＿＿＿

Using Your Words:

Sound-alike words

tease\tees\teas
some\sum
choose\chews

Use a dictionary to find the meanings of these words. Write them in sentences with other words on your spelling list.

_____

_____

_____

_____

_____

_____

_____

_____

_____

Spelling Lesson:

As you hear them, write the spelling words for the day in the space provided. Be sure that you correct any words you have spelled incorrectly.

1._____

2._____

3._____

4._____

5._____

6._____

7._____

8._____

9._____

10. _____

11. _____

12. _____

13. _____

14. _____

15. _____

16. _____

17. _____

18. _____

19._____

20. _____

21. _____

22. _____

23. _____

24. _____

25. _____

Using Your Words:

Fill in the blanks with words from today's spelling list.

1. That furniture arrangement is very _____ to the eye.

2. What a _____ way to spend the afternoon.

3. My day was full of _____.

4. Here _____ Jake and Lisa.

5. The color yellow _____ you.

6. Is there _____ special you would like for your birthday?

7. _____, I would like to travel to Egypt.

8. Are _____ your gloves? Whose are _____?

9. Please take _____ to Lisa.

Day 159

As you hear them, write the spelling words for the day in the space provided. Be sure that you correct any words you have spelled incorrectly.

1. _____

2. _____

3. _____

4. _____

5. _____

6. _____

7. _____

8. _____

9. _____

10. _____

11. _____

12. _____

13. _____

14. _____

15. _____

16. _____

17. _____

18. _____

19. _____

20. _____

21. _____

22. _____

23. _____

24. _____

25. _____

Using Your Words:

Unscramble these:

1. teesa _____

2. epladse _____

3. urplsesae _____

4. tnpaasle _____

5. steeh _____

6. uipssrser _____

7. yomsoedb _____

8. ssmeemtio _____

9. roorme _____

10. romur _____

Day 160

Spelling Lesson:

As you hear them, write the spelling words for the day in the space provided. Be sure that you correct any words you have spelled incorrectly.

1._____

2._____

3._____

4._____

5._____

6._____

7._____

8._____

9._____

10. _____

11. _____

12. _____

13. _____

14. _____

15. _____

16. _____

17. _____

18. _____

19._____

20. _____

21. _____

22. _____

23. _____

24. _____

25. _____

Using Your Words:

Choose at least seven words from your spelling list and use them in a short paragraph, silly story or poem.

_____

_____

_____

_____

_____

_____

_____

_____

_____

_____

Evaluation Test #4

1. Only a pig takes up two parking sp_____.

2. His only adv_____ was to be true to yourself.

3. There are too many g_____ in our neighborhood.

4. How many ch_____ do you want to make?

5. Who was that str_____ wearing the mask?

6. I hate to hear about someone getting m_____.

7. I hope you're just k_____ me.

8. My sister is always h_____ her things from me.

9. It g_____ with the territory.

10. One hundred is just one with two zer_____after it.

11. Sarah says she d_____ ever want to get married.

12. We were not all_____ to go.

13. They are sl_____ down.

14. We'll be back after the foll_____.

15. Will you pl_____ close the door behind you.

16. I enjoy eating shr_____ wheat for breakfast.

17. I enjoy taking a sn_____ right after supper.

18. I love to see the flowers in bl_____.

19. You're welc_____.

20. She was overc_____ with grief.

Day 161

As you hear them, write the spelling words for the day in the space provided. Be sure that you correct any words you have spelled incorrectly.

1._____

2._____

3._____

4._____

5._____

6._____

7._____

8._____

9._____

10. _____

11. _____

12. _____

13. _____

14. _____

15. _____

16. _____

17. _____

18. _____

19._____

20. _____

21. _____

22. _____

23. _____

24. _____

25. _____

Using Your Words:

List as many words as you can that have the following letters (in order) in them.

edge

oth

rth

Day 162

Spelling Lesson:

As you hear them, write the spelling words for the day in the space provided. Be sure that you correct any words you have spelled incorrectly.

1._____

2._____

3._____

4._____

5._____

6._____

7._____

8._____

9._____

10. _____

11. _____

12. _____

13. _____

14. _____

15. _____

16. _____

17. _____

18. _____

19._____

20. _____

21. _____

22. _____

23. _____

24. _____

25. _____

Using Your Words:

Fill in the blanks with words from today's spelling list.

1. _____ is one of the planets in the solar system.

2. How many _____ does your sleeping compartment have?

3. I need to get my _____ cleaned today.

4. Did you lose your front _____?

5. Sometimes, taking a deep _____ will help you to stay calm.

6. I was sorry to learn of your father's _____.

7. We stood at the _____ of the canyon and looked down.

8. Will _____ of you be coming for dinner?

Day 163

Spelling Lesson:

As you hear them, write the spelling words for the day in the space provided. Be sure that you correct any words you have spelled incorrectly.

1._____

2._____

3._____

4._____

5._____

6._____

7._____

8._____

9._____

10. _____

11. _____

12. _____

13. _____

14. _____

15. _____

16. _____

17. _____

18. _____

19._____

20. _____

21. _____

22. _____

23. _____

24. _____

25. _____

Using Your Words:

Unscramble these:

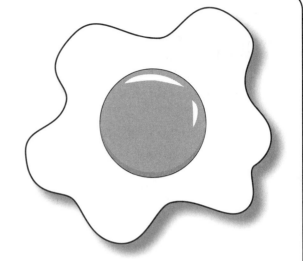

1. eetnrhdau _____

2. atdriybh _____

3. horbohustt _____

4. urhtt _____

5. ohtb _____

6. reblsshaet _____

7. adeht _____

8. sbgadre _____

9. pegdeld _____

10. dnoweclkagde _____

Day 164

Spelling Lesson:

As you hear them, write the spelling words for the day in the space provided. Be sure that you correct any words you have spelled incorrectly.

1._____

2._____

3._____

4._____

5._____

6._____

7._____

8._____

9._____

10. _____

11. _____

12. _____

13. _____

14. _____

15. _____

16. _____

17. _____

18. _____

19._____

20. _____

21. _____

22. _____

23. _____

24. _____

25. _____

Using Your Words:

Write a sentence using the following words:

1. birth _____

_____

2. berth _____

_____

3. breathlessly _____

_____

4. truth _____

_____

5. breathing _____

_____

6. youthfulness _____

_____

7. tollbooth _____

_____

Day 165

As you hear them, write the spelling words for the day in the space provided. Be sure that you correct any words you have spelled incorrectly.

1._____

2._____

3._____

4._____

5._____

6._____

7._____

8._____

9._____

10. _____

11. _____

12. _____

13. _____

14. _____

15. _____

16. _____

17. _____

18. _____

19._____

20. _____

21. _____

22. _____

23. _____

24. _____

25. _____

Using Your Words:

Sound-alike words

lie\lye; die\dye
eye\I\aye
by\buy\bye

Use a dictionary to find the meanings of these words. Write them in sentences with other words on your spelling list.

1._____

_____

2._____

_____

3._____

_____

4._____

_____

5._____

_____

6._____

_____

7._____

_____

8._____

_____

9._____

_____

10._____

_____

Day 166

Spelling Lesson:

As you hear them, write the spelling words for the day in the space provided. Be sure that you correct any words you have spelled incorrectly.

1._____

2._____

3._____

4._____

5._____

6._____

7._____

8._____

9._____

10._____

11._____

12._____

13._____

14._____

15._____

16._____

17._____

18._____

19._____

20._____

21._____

22._____

23._____

24._____

25._____

Using Your Words:

List as many words as you can that have the following letters (in order) in them.

ie

ye

y

_____

_____

_____

_____

_____

_____

_____

_____

Day 167

As you hear them, write the spelling words for the day in the space provided. Be sure that you correct any words you have spelled incorrectly.

1. _____

2. _____

3. _____

4. _____

5. _____

6. _____

7. _____

8. _____

9. _____

10. _____

11. _____

12. _____

13. _____

14. _____

15. _____

16. _____

17. _____

18. _____

19. _____

20. _____

21. _____

22. _____

23. _____

24. _____

25. _____

Using Your Words:

Fill in the blanks with words from today's spelling list.

1. Do you like your _____ pan-_____ or deep-

_____?

2. I _____ to stop the tears, but I still _____.

3. The robber _____ open the window.

4. She _____ about her age.

5. The avalanche _____ several large boulders.

6. Lisa is a bl_____-_____ blonde.

7. Allison is a br_____-_____ brunette.

8. Susan d_____ her sheets yellow.

Day 168

Spelling Lesson:

As you hear them, write the spelling words for the day in the space provided. Be sure that you correct any words you have spelled incorrectly.

1._____

2._____

3._____

4._____

5._____

6._____

7._____

8._____

9._____

10. _____

11. _____

12. _____

13. _____

14. _____

15. _____

16. _____

17. _____

18. _____

19._____

20. _____

21. _____

22. _____

23. _____

24. _____

25. _____

Using Your Words:

Can you find the words?

```
X E R M F K D R M S E M G U J
O W Y E Y O Z J S Y S L N E Z
R H S B D E L E E D E K I Y E
F I W G D M R D Z Y I I E J X
U I I Z L O E E D Q R K Y O A
Q N R D N R O R H F P X D L I
G I N M J F F G T W A R Y Z Z
E D B K X C R S R X D I H O V
S R E G D O L Y Y E N G H N H
N D C R Y I N G I G N A F L Q
U V B K R O X R N N H J C Z B
C A A U N C T X G X G F E P L
U W K T F Z E E D Y C E Y J O
T M E G X G N I Y D O P O O F
W W H E N E P T T D B P P T A
```

Words Used

crying

dodging

dyeing

dying

frying

goodbye

lodgers

lying

pries

redeye

tried

trying

when

where

Spelling Lesson:

As you hear them, write the spelling words for the day in the space provided. Be sure that you correct any words you have spelled incorrectly.

1._____

2._____

3._____

4._____

5._____

6._____

7._____

8._____

9._____

10. _____

11. _____

12. _____

13. _____

14. _____

15. _____

16. _____

17. _____

18. _____

19._____

20. _____

21. _____

22. _____

23. _____

24. _____

25. _____

Using Your Words:

Fill in the blanks with words from today's spelling list.

1. Where did you _____ for a job?

2. I hope I can _____ on you to complete the project on time.

3. Do spiders _____ you?

4. Let's go back to the _____.

5. Our company must _____ with the EPA regulations.

6. Why did she _____ the request?

7. I would really appreciate a _____ as soon as possible.

8. Britain is a key _____ of the United States.

Day 170

As you hear them, write the spelling words for the day in the space provided. Be sure that you correct any words you have spelled incorrectly.

1._____

2._____

3._____

4._____

5._____

6._____

7._____

8._____

9._____

10. _____

11. _____

12. _____

13. _____

14. _____

15. _____

16. _____

17. _____

18. _____

19._____

20. _____

21. _____

22. _____

23. _____

24. _____

25. _____

Using Your Words:

Unscramble these:

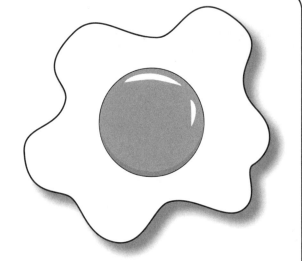

1. spise   _____

2. suesiplp   _____

3. ipmiullste   _____

4. . rleesi   _____

5. sstsifideais   _____

6. frrshoiei   _____

7. nbiigngen   _____

8. . ieflsoiids   _____

9. erriiefts   _____

10. ginnwsin   _____

Spelling Lesson:

As you hear them, write the spelling words for the day in the space provided. Be sure that you correct any words you have spelled incorrectly.

1._____

2._____

3._____

4._____

5._____

6._____

7._____

8._____

9._____

10. _____

11. _____

12. _____

13. _____

14. _____

15. _____

16. _____

17. _____

18. _____

19._____

20. _____

21. _____

22. _____

23. _____

24. _____

25. _____

Using Your Words:

List as many words as you can that have the following letters (in order) in them.

nner

_____

_____

_____

_____

_____

_____

_____

_____

_____

Day 172

As you hear them, write the spelling words for the day in the space provided. Be sure that you correct any words you have spelled incorrectly.

1._____

2._____

3._____

4._____

5._____

6._____

7._____

8._____

9._____

10. _____

11. _____

12. _____

13. _____

14. _____

15. _____

16. _____

17. _____

18. _____

19._____

20. _____

21. _____

22. _____

23. _____

24. _____

25. _____

Using Your Words:

Choose at least seven words from your spelling list and use them in a short paragraph, silly story or poem.

_____

_____

_____

_____

_____

_____

_____

_____

_____

_____

Day 173

As you hear them, write the spelling words for the day in the space provided. Be sure that you correct any words you have spelled incorrectly.

1._____

2._____

3._____

4._____

5._____

6._____

7._____

8._____

9._____

10. _____

11. _____

12. _____

13. _____

14. _____

15. _____

16. _____

17. _____

18. _____

19._____

20. _____

21. _____

22. _____

23. _____

24. _____

25. _____

Using Your Words:

List as many words as you can that have the following letters (in order) in them.

atter

oak

oll

_____

_____

_____

_____

_____

_____

_____

_____

_____

Day 174

Spelling Lesson:

As you hear them, write the spelling words for the day in the space provided. Be sure that you correct any words you have spelled incorrectly.

1._____

2._____

3._____

4._____

5._____

6._____

7._____

8._____

9._____

10. _____

11. _____

12. _____

13. _____

14. _____

15. _____

16. _____

17. _____

18. _____

19._____

20. _____

21. _____

22. _____

23. _____

24. _____

25. _____

Using Your Words:

Sound-alike words

boy\buoy
boll\bow
roll\role

Look alike words: **live** "liv" or "l'YH'z"
lives "livz" or "l'YHvz"
Use each of these words correctly in a sentence.

1._____

_____

2._____

_____

3._____

_____

4._____

_____

5._____

_____

6._____

_____

7._____

_____

8._____

_____

Day 175

Spelling Lesson:

As you hear them, write the spelling words for the day in the space provided. Be sure that you correct any words you have spelled incorrectly.

1. _____

2. _____

3. _____

4. _____

5. _____

6. _____

7. _____

8. _____

9. _____

10. _____

11. _____

12. _____

13. _____

14. _____

15. _____

16. _____

17. _____

18. _____

19. _____

20. _____

21. _____

22. _____

23. _____

24. _____

25. _____

Using Your Words:

Fill in the blanks with words from today's spelling list.

1. _____ that Lisa's sister, Debbie?

2. Do you have the _____ for this flashlight?

3. Wow! He really _____ his bat.

4. Did you buy your sister a new _____?

5. I get _____ when you whine.

6. _____ you finished yet?

7. He _____ a perfect game.

8. _____ you please join me for lunch?

9. Jon _____ the flowers to the hospital.

10. We I _____ on Pearl Street for nine years.

Day 176

As you hear them, write the spelling words for the day in the space provided. Be sure that you correct any words you have spelled incorrectly.

1._____

2._____

3._____

4._____

5._____

6._____

7._____

8._____

9._____

10. _____

11. _____

12. _____

13. _____

14. _____

15. _____

16. _____

17. _____

18. _____

19._____

20. _____

21. _____

22. _____

23. _____

24. _____

25. _____

Using Your Words:

Can you find the words?

M	I	K	K	C	S	U	W	H	U	V	M	Q	M	S
V	I	S	O	Y	B	M	R	O	Q	U	W	W	G	O
M	D	D	E	R	E	T	T	A	P	S	F	F	N	A
U	W	R	Y	G	E	S	J	J	K	D	L	T	I	K
S	V	S	B	R	N	B	L	Q	J	A	O	B	L	E
X	H	G	A	O	D	I	N	I	T	U	O	U	L	D
O	I	A	T	I	G	A	Y	T	V	W	J	D	O	A
X	W	N	T	S	S	J	E	O	L	E	E	U	R	A
X	P	Q	E	T	X	R	Y	E	L	R	R	P	T	Z
L	A	M	R	Y	E	P	D	O	E	P	N	S	S	H
U	F	Z	I	D	F	R	C	V	F	S	M	F	E	P
S	D	D	E	V	I	L	I	O	F	O	E	E	V	A
Y	X	C	S	V	H	L	X	N	G	F	C	V	A	O
T	L	L	E	V	E	F	O	R	G	A	V	E	I	S
S	H	Y	Y	D	M	V	A	W	G	E	J	B	M	L

Words Used

batteries

bowled

delivered

employing

flattered

forgave

lived

lives

shattering

slivers

soaked

soap

spattered

strolling

Day 177

Spelling Lesson:

As you hear them, write the spelling words for the day in the space provided. Be sure that you correct any words you have spelled incorrectly.

1._____

2._____

3._____

4._____

5._____

6._____

7._____

8._____

9._____

10. _____

11. _____

12. _____

13. _____

14. _____

15. _____

16. _____

17. _____

18. _____

19._____

20. _____

21. _____

22. _____

23. _____

24. _____

25. _____

Using Your Words:

List as many words as you can that have the following letters (in order) in them.

ook

ool

ace

_____

_____

_____

_____

_____

_____

_____

_____

_____

Spelling Lesson:

As you hear them, write the spelling words for the day in the space provided. Be sure that you correct any words you have spelled incorrectly.

1._____

2._____

3._____

4._____

5._____

6._____

7._____

8._____

9._____

10. _____

11. _____

12. _____

13. _____

14. _____

15. _____

16. _____

17. _____

18. _____

19._____

20. _____

21. _____

22. _____

23. _____

24. _____

25. _____

Using Your Words:

Sound-alike words

band\banned
chased\chaste
baste\based

Use each of these words correctly in a sentence.

1._____

_____

2._____

_____

3._____

_____

4._____

_____

5._____

_____

6._____

_____

Sequential Spelling Level 1 - Student Workbook

Day 179

Spelling Lesson:

As you hear them, write the spelling words for the day in the space provided. Be sure that you correct any words you have spelled incorrectly.

1._____

2._____

3._____

4._____

5._____

6._____

7._____

8._____

9._____

10. _____

11. _____

12. _____

13. _____

14. _____

15. _____

16. _____

17. _____

18. _____

19._____

20. _____

21. _____

22. _____

23. _____

24. _____

25. _____

Using Your Words

Fill in the blanks with words from today's spelling list.

1. I _____ decided if I'll come along.

2. Are you _____ visitors later?

3. The dog _____ the ball that I threw.

4. My dad's company is _____ in New Hampshire, so he travels there often.

5. Please bring me a _____ for these flowers.

6. Your _____ played that song well.

7. _____ you please bring along a _____ to read?

8. _____ can be scratchy.

Day 180

As you hear them, write the spelling words for the day in the space provided. Be sure that you correct any words you have spelled incorrectly.

1._____

2._____

3._____

4._____

5._____

6._____

7._____

8._____

9._____

10._____

11._____

12._____

13._____

14._____

15._____

16._____

17._____

18._____

19._____

20._____

21._____

22._____

23._____

24._____

25._____

Using Your Words:

Choose at least seven words from your spelling list and use them in a short paragraph, silly story or poem.

_____

_____

_____

_____

_____

_____

_____

_____

_____

_____

Final Evaluation Test

1. Let's go back to the very beg_____.

2. Let's not get into a sh_____ match.

3. I'm pl_____ on having a good vacation.

4. I hate to have spl_____headaches.

5. My flashlight needs a new b_____.

6. They are bu_____ a new house.

7. It's a very l_____ puppy.

8. The wind was bl_____ hard.

9. We were l_____ the truck.

10. Tom st_____ behind to watch the house.

11. He is m_____ to his own drummer.

12. They raise sheep and g_____.

13. I am dep_____ upon you.

14. He dem_____ to know who I was.

15. The basketball game was really exc_____.

16. We are h_____ them over for dinner.

17. He rec_____ how it was when he was a kid.

18. Put the package up on the sh_____.

19. I love the thr_____ and the sp_____.

20. Never carry a conc_____ weapon.

21. The pr_____ remained the same all day.

22. We just ch_____ the oil last week.

Story Starters

Sometimes, pictures can inspire us to write poems or stories. Take a look at the picture above. What do you think happened before and after? Has something similar happened to you? How did you react? Think about these questions as you write a short poem or story about this picture.

Story Starters

Sometimes, pictures can inspire us to write poems or stories. Take a look at the picture above. What do you think happened before and after? Has something similar happened to you? How did you react? Think about these questions as you write a short poem or story about this picture.

Story Starters

Sometimes, pictures can inspire us to write poems or stories. Take a look at the picture above. What do you think happened before and after? Has something similar happened to you? How did you react? Think about these questions as you write a short poem or story about this picture.

Story Starters

Sometimes, pictures can inspire us to write poems or stories. Take a look at the picture above. What do you think happened before and after? Has something similar happened to you? How did you react? Think about these questions as you write a short poem or story about this picture.